"Call 'Playa' Hater!"

Kwame Ronnie Vanderhorst

•

Cover art by Jomo Howard Bullard
Author's photo by Myron Ottley

ISBN 0-9652104-6-4

HOTEP PRODUCTIONS

To book Kwame Ronnie Vanderhorst or for additional information to
order his books, tapes and materials, contact:
Prepare Our Youth, Inc.
6856 Eastern Avenue NW Suite 207
Washington, D.C. 20012
(202) 291-5040 (202) 291-5042 fax
www.poyinc.org

Dedicated

*In memory of all the youngins who
"played" but to adulthood never made.
Rest In Peace*

Playa'
1982 - 1999

"Shout Outs!"

Onyamee Kwame - The Creator
Stevan Vanderhorst
Jomo Howard Bullard
Shantell "Shanny" Lewis
Emmanuel-Brinklow Youth
Prepare Our Youth Supporters

Table Of Contents

I'M NOT CRITICIZIN', BUT I DO CRITIQUE, THA MAN GOT YOUNGINS TRIPPIN' DOWN FAKE STREET. GENIUS ENSLAVED, FUTURE INTERRUPTED, POTENTIAL CORRUPTED, YOUR VISION BLURRED.

THONG SONGS, PACKIN' NINES, BLUNTIN' UP DREAMS - RECOGNIZE - CORPORATE PIMPS SCOPED YOU, HOLLYWOOD DOPED YOU, COPS BEATIN' YOU DOWN, BLOOD WATERS THE GROUND, SPREADIN' AIDS, MAKIN' MAD MONEY, FUNERALS EVERYDAY, PIMP-SLAPPIN' YO' HONEY!

DISRESPECTIN' ELDERS, DRESSIN' IN STYLE, WHILE THE FATHERLESS CHILD IS RUNNIN' WILD! I'M NOT CRITICIZIN', BUT I DO CRITIQUE, THA MAN GOT YOUNGINS TRIPPIN' DOWN FAKE STREET.

I KICK A MELANIN FLOW, TO LIBERATE YOUR MIND, SO TRUTH CAN EDUCATE YOU, WISDOM PROTECT YOU, HOPE INSPIRE YOU, OUR CREATOR GUIDE YOU, KNOWLEDGE CLOTHE YOU, LOVE INFOLD YOU, PRAYER TRANSFORM YOU, AND RESPECT CROWN YOU.

CALL ME A PLAYA' HATER, BUT YOU'LL FEEL ME LATER!

Preface

One of the most popular and often asked question by many youth today is, **"Why you playa' hatin'?** This question has a broad range of implications, such as, "Why are you - jealous, envious, mad, insecure or trippin'?" Saying that a person is *playa' hatin'* is insinuating that that person is responding inappropriately - that they are disapproving, jealous, critical or envious of the actions of a so-called playa'.

The popular response to the question, "Why you playa' hatin'" is, **"Don't hate the playa, hate the game!"** Playa' hatin' is tantamount to irreverence, as if a so-called playa' is never to be challenged, critiqued, questioned or disagreed with! Well, this is my response to all that: **CALL ME A PLAYA' HATER!** In fact, if you keep reading, you'll find out just what I'm hatin'! In the meantime, analyze this:

- **Is a playa' still a playa' after the physician says, "AIDS?"**
- **Is a playa' still a playa after the judge says, 'Life without parole?"**
- **Is a playa' still a playa' after he sees his own wayward son or daughter he never took care of in a casket?**
- **Is a playa' still a playa' after your mama gets her car or home confiscated because you were busted selling drugs?**

And you're still wondering why I'm a playa' hater? At least you won't be able to say I didn't say anything - that I didn't care. I'm giving my "cut" (perspective) on some of the negativity I see in Hip-Hop culture. If you listen, you will learn how to live a healthy and productive life.

Here is my objective in a nutshell: **First, I'm gonna critique your beliefs and behavior. Next, I'm gonna challenge your perspectives and practices. Finally, I'm gonna question your attitudes and actions.**

It takes **conviction, character,** and **conduct** to arrive at adulthood - physically, mentally, spiritually, socially and culturally equipped. In short, I just want you **to know, to be, and to do.** But time is of the essence! Why?

"The day is fast, the time is late, it's a dangerous thing to make one mistake. The earth is in a five o'clock rush, Babylon is here with confusion as such. Men and women both look alike, Truth and Lie are having a fight. The wise are called foolish and the foolish are called wise. People are living in many disguise. Words and voices are at their peak, woe to he or she who's still asleep. The day is fast, the time is late, it's a dangerous thing to make one mistake!" (Poem by Stephen E. Patterson)

Introduction

Picture this: I'm kickin' it with Youngin and his honey. We're at brunch. I look over at two guys and their honey's sitting at a table on the other side of the restaurant. They finish eating and get up. The chubby dude tears up the bill, drops it on the floor, and they walk out without paying. The young sista at the cash register is afraid to call her manager and report them. She cusses under her breath because it's gonna come out of her pay!

Me (Kwame): "Ya'll see that?"

Youngin: "Yeah."

Kwame: "They trippin!"

Youngin: "Why you playa' hatin'?"

Kwame: "I'm glad you asked! I been dyin' to get this out! Ya'll got anywhere to go?"

Youngin: "Nah, we cool." (Youngin puts his fork down, crosses his arms, and looks me straight in the eyes. His honey keeps eating, but she's all ears.)

Kwame: "I've been trying to hit upon something to compare Hip-hop culture with. I think I found it."

Youngin: "What is it?"

Kwame: "Religion! Hip-Hop culture is the religion of this young generation. I know some elders in our community would think I'm being sacrilegious for saying that, but hip-hop is as pervasive as religion. Hip-Hop is not a fad - a flash in the pan - like in the '60's when afros and dashikis were the style of the day. Anyway, most of them eventually cut their hair (or lost it), put on Armani and Ann Klein suits and are now supporting the same oppressive system they once fought to change. But that's another book.

Hip-Hop culture is here to stay! Like religion, it may change some of its rituals, but the structure will stay in tact. Check it out. Hip-Hop has its membership and leaders who come and go. And like religion, there is a lot of "hipocrisy" (my word) in Hip-Hop culture. They call lying, robbing, killing and stealing, *"keepin' it real!"* If that ain't hipocrisy, breaths don't stink!"

Youngin: "I feel you. Go on."

Kwame: "My friend and brother in the struggle to educate and empower youth, Dr. Dwayne Nosakhere Thomas, has studied Hip-Hop culture. This is what he said: *"As I have researched, studied and lectured on Hip-Hop culture, I have come to define it as an African-originated, music-centered, rebelliously assertive cultural voice of urban African American youth. This culture is shaped by the language, fashions, hair styles, and worldwide view of a generation alienated not only from the eurocentric dominant culture, but to a surprising degree from its traditional African heritage, as it relates to cultural-religious values. However, from the standpoint of counter-cultural that shocks, it's no different from the voice of previous generations."*

Youngin: "Most grown-ups think Hip-Hop is just gangsta rap music. Wrong! Is religion just gospel music? No! Doc, hit on it when he included language, fashions, hair styles, but he forgot hoochies!" (His honey smiles, punches him in the arm and says, "I ain't nobody's hoochie!")

Youngin: "You my hoochie, and you know it!" (They laugh).

Kwame: "You was cool 'til you said, "hoochies." That's another reason why I'm playa' hatin'! But I'll get with the language later. As I was about to say, Dr. Thomas says that this generation, *"Through their music and behaviors are crying out to express themselves culturally, socially and politically. The messages in their music and their cultural expression, all suggest a reaction to perceived ills and real deficits in mainstream society. This voice is expressing rage and pain; the pain evident in the statistics regarding what Generation X experiences."*

Kwame: "Some adults say you are a 'lost' generation. Well if your generation is 'lost,' then my generation lost you! We are *responsible* for that. My generation must be responsible enough to change the societal conditions that we have created that you must live in. But your generation must be held *accountable* for your negative choices and decisions. My generation and your generation got to work it out together."

Dr. Thomas concludes: "*Hip-Hop has become the value basis that informs the decision-making process of our youth. In each instance above, the positive value is negated by an overriding negative value, and because these negative values are so thoroughly ingrained into hip-hop music/culture, it is almost impossible for a young person inundated with these messages to glean a positive impact upon his/her mind and decision-making faculties.*" Dr. Thomas calls this chart the "*value system of hip-hop.*"

Positive	Negative
Self-definition	Substance Abuse
Creativity	Gang-orientation
Ebonics (Black English)	Vulgarity
Black Consciousness	Degrading Blacks
Community-orientation	Degrading Women
Self-reliance	Disrespect for Authority
Self-perseverance	Short -life Expectancy
Intelligence	Prison-informed
Economic Empowerment	Gambling
Musical Genius	Sex-obsession
Africentrism	Masculine Women
Self-determination	Rebellion
Political Awareness /	Violence
Black rage	

Kwame: "I'm puttin' my scope on some of the negatives of Hip-Hop culture and analyzing their effects on young people. **Hip-Hop culture can be a powerful tool for mass youth mobilization, socially responsible advocacy and activism, as well as, academic and moral excellence among youth. But the negatives keep Hip-Hop culture from reaching its true prophetic potential.**

In my book, I'm not criticizing, but I do critique. Critique is not the same as criticism. Criticism is destructive - period. Critique is constructive and offers viable suggestions. A lot of young people don't like to be checked. They play it off by calling the person a *playa' hater*. The truth is that some of them want to avoid anyone who will question their lifestyle, choices and behavior. They live on the defensive. It's them against the world! They try to act strong but in reality they're weak, because they fear critique.

Critique gives you an opportunity to examine yourself, your lifestyle, your choices and your associations. Critique gives you an opportunity to close your loopholes. If you are not strong enough to handle critique, then you will never mature."

Youngin: "I like kickin' it with you, brotha Kwame, although I like brunch better!" (Laugh). I tell you what, you give me your playa' hatin' book and I'll read it. Better yet, I'll let my "hoochie" read it to me while I chill and listen."

Youngin's Honey: (Talking loud) "Who you think I am, 'Hooked On Phonics' or somethin'? It ain't my fault you can't read good. If you put a book in your face as much as you put those plugs in your ears, you wouldn't be askin' me to read to you." (Rollin' her eyes at him!)

Youngin: "Now YOU playa' hatin' Shorty!" (He acts like he's choking her as we get up to leave - they're laughing). "You still payin' Brother Kwame?"

Kwame: "No! I'm gonna tear up the check and we walkin' out like those other youngins!"

Youngin: "NOW YOU A PLAYA'! (Youngin smilin', showing his gold tooth!)

Kwame: "Sike! I'm payin'. I'm not a fake thug like those youngins'. Besides, *what goes around comes around!*"

It is my prayer that his book will be part of your collective solutions. Hotep.

Kwame Ronnie Vanderhorst

(Playa' Hater #1)

Booty Call!

"When I saw him, I wanted to know him. And when I knew him, I wanted to love him. And when I loved him, I gave him my all. And when I gave him my all, I got infected!"

Our Creator gave humans an innate, natural desire for normal sexual activity. At a certain age, hormones secrete into our blood system, and physical/emotional changes begin to happen in our bodies. Hair begins to grow around the penis and vagina. Guys get hard-ons. Testicles start filling up with sperm and become supersensitive. Girls begin to bud breasts. Menstruation (periods) starts. But it's all good. It's our Creator's natural way of preparing humans to procreate.

Sexual intercourse, is most mutually fulfilling and safest when a male and female are married and monogamous. Sexual intercourse becomes very risky outside of a monogamous marriage. I made this statement in my book, *Smellin' Ourselves: What Men Need To Understand About Our Women*:

"In our Creator's divine plan for human existence, man was not complete until woman was created. In this, and no other relationship, can human procreation, progeny, or society exist or continue. There is no so-called alternate lifestyle that can accomplish this fact. The male-female relationship is the most complimentary natural order of human existence. Male-female relationships are the highest expression of our Creator's oneness on earth."

Unfortunately, youngins are becoming sexually aware, and some, sexually active sooner than later. The corporate-controlled media (t.v., video, movie, music, magazines and Internet) has increased our exposure to sexually explicit offerings. An abundance of sexually explicit material is so accessible to children and youth today that we don't even have to leave our homes to be seduced by it.

To be fair, sexual promiscuity is not new. It's old school. It's been around almost as long as humans. In fact, the sexual obsession expressed in Hip-Hop culture is simply the byproduct of the sexually-obsessed society we are living in.

Choices or Consequences

When I talk about Booty Call, I'm referring to a pervasive mentality in Hip-Hop culture (and society) that endorses, encourages and engages in illicit sexual activity. The adage is, "sex sells." But at who's expense? If sex sells, then somebody's paying for it!

Here's the main point I want you to know about Booty Call: **You have control over your *choices*, but what you don't have control over is the *consequences*!** It's either healthy choices or unhealthy consequences! And the consequences of Booty Call are awesome!

Because of Booty Call, there are hundreds of thousands of young people who are HIV positive - and many of them don't know it - yet - and because they don't know it, they are going to make a lot more young people HIV positive! I haven't even mentioned other STDs that so many young people have contracted!

After the gift of love, I believe the second greatest gift our Creator has given us is *choice*. We are not robots. We can choose. With choice comes power. There are two things that happen psychologically when you make a choice. First, the issue is settled for the moment. Second, you are more likely to make a similar choice the next time. Making the same choice over and over again becomes a habit.

Virtue, abstinence, and deferred gratification are good choices. When you choose to live a virtuous life, you will be tempted sexually, but if you choose to abstain, you will get stronger and more resolute in remaining clean. But if you surrender your choice to someone else's choice, you lose your power. Should you not choose abstinence and make a Booty Call, you immediately move into the realm of consequences! The consequences are out of your control! Syphilis, chlamydia, gonorrhea, herpes, genital warts, or HIV and AIDS are vicious!

You should never ever have to experience any of these consequences. And these are just consequences on your health. The mental-emotional toll they take on an infected person is just as vicious! And if you don't have a good support system to assist you through these consequences, all I can say is, "Lord have mercy on you!"

Premarital sexual activity may be good *to* you but it is not good *for* you. Premarital (or extramarital) sexual activity cannot offer the mental-emotional and spiritually rewarding benefits that it can within a faithful marriage. There are too many *consequences* associated with premarital and extramarital sexual activity. Today, Booty Call is more dangerous than it's ever been! It can even be deadly!

I'm gonna drop some knowledge so you can use it to stay healthy and stay alive. As I write this book, I presently manage a program that addresses HIV/AIDS and substance abuse in nine public schools in Washington, D.C. The objective of the program is is to reduce the spread of HIV and substance abuse among middle school and high school students through prevention education. Let me educate you to the perils of Booty Call.

Early Symptoms of HIV

The Human Immuno-deficiency Virus (HIV) is a virus that weakens the immune systems and causes Acquired Immuno-Deficiency Syndrome (AIDS). A person does not get AIDS – they get the HIV virus. HIV causes AIDS.

HIV is spread most commonly by sexual contact with an infected partner. The virus can enter the body through the lining of the vagina, vulva, penis, rectum or mouth during sexual intercourse. HIV is also spread through contact with infected blood. HIV frequently is spread among injection drug users by the sharing of needles or syringes contaminated with minute quantities of blood of someone infected with the virus.

Women can transmit HIV to their fetuses during pregnancy or birth. Approximately one-quarter to one-third of all untreated pregnant women infected with HIV will pass the infection to their babies. HIV also can be spread to babies through the breast milk of mothers infected with the virus. Today, African American children are the second fastest growing group of people to become infected with HIV/AIDS next to the African American heterosexual woman.

Many people do not develop any symptoms when they first become infected with HIV. Some people, have a flu-like illness within a month or two after exposure to the virus. They may have fever, headache, malaise and enlarged lymph nodes (organs of the immune system easily felt in the neck and groin). These symptoms usually disappear within a week to a month and are often mistaken for those of another viral infection. People are very infectious during this period, and HIV is present in large quantities in genital secretions.

Some people may begin to have symptoms in as soon as a few months, whereas others may be symptom-free for more than 10 years. During these "symptom-free" years, however, HIV is actively multiplying, infecting and killing cells of the immune system. HIV's effect is seen most obviously in a decline in the blood levels of CD4+ T cells (also called T4 cells) – the immune system's key infection fighters. The virus initially disables or destroys these cells without causing symptoms.

As the immune system deteriorates, a variety of complications begin to surface. One of the first such symptoms experienced by many people infected with HIV is large lymph nodes or "swollen glands" that may be enlarged for more than three months. Other symptoms often experienced months to years before the onset of AIDS include the lack of energy, weight loss, frequent fevers and sweats, persistent or frequent yeast infections (oral or vaginal), persistent skin rash or flaky skin, pelvic inflammatory disease that does not respond to treatment, or short term memory loss.

AIDS

AIDS stands for, Acquired Immuno-Deficiency Syndrome. The term AIDS applies to the most advanced stages of HIV infection. The Centers for Disease Control (CDC) defined AIDS to include all HIV-infected people who have fewer than 200 T4 cells. Most recently CDC's definition of AIDS include all HIV-infected people who have fewer than 500 T4 cells. Healthy adults usually have a T4 cell counts of 1,000 or more. (If you are around 500 in your T4 cell count, you are considered at stage one. A T4 cell count in the range of 200-499 is stage two. A T4 cell count below 200 is considered stage three.)

In people with AIDS, **opportunistic infections** may be fatal because the immune system is so ravaged by HIV that the body cannot fight off certain bacteria, viruses and other microbe. Opportunistic infections common in people with AIDS cause such symptoms as:

• *Coughing*: A dry cough lasting several days or longer, in the absence of an illness such as a cold
• *Shortness of breath*
• *Persistent fever*: Prolonged temperature of 99-101 degrees in the absence of an illness such as the flu
• *Severe and persistent diarrhea*: Runny bowel movements that occur several times daily repeatedly for many weeks
• *Extreme fatigue*: Chronic tiredness during regular daily activities, despite plenty of sleep
• *Weight loss*: Loss of 10 pounds or more without dieting or change in regular intake of food
• *Swollen glands*: Enlarged lymph glands in the neck, groin, or armpit. May be sore or tender
• *Night sweats*: Sweats that soak the bed sheets, with or without a fever
• *Skin rash*: Itchy bumps or ulcers appearing anywhere on the body; they often spread
• *Oral problems*: Sores or white patches (thrush) on the gums, tongue, or palate

Other problems are, *vision loss, severe headaches, nausea, vomiting, lack of coordination, coma, abdominal cramps, difficult or painful swallowing, seizures,* and *mental symptoms such as confusion and forgetfulness*

Many people are so debilitated by the symptoms of AIDS that they are unable to hold steady employment or do household chores. Other people with AIDS may experience phases of intense life-threatening illness followed by phases of normal functioning.

People exposed to HIV should be tested for HIV infection as soon as they are likely to develop antibodies to the virus. Such early testing will enable them to receive appropriate treatment at a time when they are most able to combat HIV and prevent the emergence of opportunistic infections. Early testing also alerts HIV-infected people to avoid high-risk behaviors that could spread HIV to others.

High Risk Behaviors

The person who has the problem is the one who doesn't know what the problem is. Once we know the problem, we can be empowered with options of resistance. There was a popular slogan back in the day that said, "If it feels good, do it!" Here again, the consequences were not taken into account. You need to know that some of the negative behaviors hyped in Hip-Hop culture place you at risk for HIV/AIDS and other nefarious consequences.

Sexual Intercourse

Many youth engage in behaviors that increase their risk of becoming HIV infected. Surveys have found that the average age for a girl in the U.S. to have sexual intercourse for the first time is 16. The average age for a boy is 15.5. It is estimated that 3 million teens are infected with sexually transmitted diseases (STDs) a year.

HIV can be spread through unprotected sexual intercourse, from male to female, female to male, or male to male. Female to female sexual transmission is possible, but rare. *Unprotected sexual intercourse means sexual intercourse without correct and consistent condom use.*

HIV may be in an infected person's blood, semen, or vaginal secretions. HIV is transmitted by vaginal, anal or oral intercourse with a person who is infected with HIV.

Drug Use

Sharing needles or syringes, even once, is an easy way to be infected with HIV. Sharing needles to inject drugs is the most dangerous form of needle sharing. Blood from an infected person can remain in or on a needle or syringe and then be transferred directly into the next person who uses it. Even the smallest amount of contaminated blood left in a used needle or syringe can be dangerous. Many females have contracted HIV by having sexual intercourse with an intravenous drug user.

Sharing Other Needles

Sharing other needles also may transmit HIV. Other needles are any needles used to puncture skin. These types of needles include:

• *Needles used to inject steroids*, which is popular with many body builders and athletes. Steroids have some permanent negative effects. Even small doses can stunt growth in young people. Prolonged use of steroids creates many health risks, including sterility, kidney failure, heart disease and cancer. Now add the latest threat - HIV infection. Because steroids weaken the immune system, you can get an infection more easily if you use them. Sharing needles with an infected teammate or body builder increases the risk of contracting HIV.

• *Needles used for tattooing.* Many youth are not getting tattooed from a qualified technician who uses sterile equipment. Bootleg tattoo artists may use the same non-sterilized needle on many people, and infected blood is transferred easily. Reputable licensed technicians will explain the safety measures they follow.

• *Needles used for body piercing* (ears, nose, tongue, navel, lips, eye brows, penis, vagina, etc.). When young people do it themselves and share needles, body piercing can pose a risk for HIV infection. Other complications may develop as a result of body piercing. Some parts of the body are very sensitive and can be easily infected after piercing if not properly cleansed.

Alcohol and Drugs
Drinking alcohol, smoking marijuana and using illegal drugs are risky behaviors. When your judgment is impaired by these substances, you are more susceptible to engage in sexual intercourse, getting raped, etc. Many have become infected because their guard was dropped through drug and alcohol use.

Ways You Cannot Get HIV/AIDS
You won't get HIV through everyday contact with infected people at school, work, home, or anywhere else. You won't get HIV from clothes, phones, bedding, swimming pools, bath tubs, hot tubs, door knobs, shaking hands, sharing clothing, or toilet seats. It can't be passed on by things like spoons, forks, cups, or other objects that someone who is infected with the virus has used. You won't get AIDS from a mosquito bite, bed bugs, lice, flies or other insects. You won't get HIV from sweat, tears, or sneezes.

You won't get HIV hugging or touching someone who is infected. You won't get HIV from a simple (dry) kiss. Experts are not completely certain about HIV transmission through deep, prolonged, or "French" kissing. The possibility exists that cuts or sores in the mouth may provide a port of entry for HIV to enter the bloodstream during prolonged deep kissing. But there has not been a single case documented in which HIV was transmitted by kissing.

Myths
• Birth control pills protect against and/or prevents HIV. **False**.
• Latex condoms prevent HIV. **False**.
Latex condoms have been shown to be highly effective in preventing HIV infection and other sexually transmitted diseases when used consistently and correctly. Latex serve as a barrier to the virus. Never use "lambskin" or "natural membrane" condoms because they have pores in them and semen or vaginal secretions can pass the virus through them. Condoms are not 100% effective. They can be defective, slip off or tear.

What To Do If You Think You Are Infected With HIV

Contact a community clinic about getting an HIV test that will determine if you are infected. What you don't know can hurt you or someone, especially if you are infected and continue to have unprotected sexual intercourse.

You can call your state or local health department. The number is under "Health Department" in the Government section of your telephone book for clinics in your city that provide free HIV testing. You can also call the CDC National AIDS Hotline (1-800-342-AIDS) to find out where you can go in your area to get counseling about an HIV test. You don't have to give your name, and the call is free.

HIV Testing

When HIV enters someone, their body tries to defend itself by making antibodies. The HIV antibodies are made slowly. There are not enough of them for blood tests to find during the first couple months of an infection.

An HIV test looks for antibodies produced by your body to fight HIV. Most people develop detectable antibodies within 3 months after infection (the average is 25 days). Testing should never take the place of prevention. HIV tests are more than 99% accurate.

A seropositive result on an HIV test means that HIV antibodies are present in your bloodstream and you are HIV positive. The HIV developing into AIDS may take up to ten or more years. Drug treatments are available that can further delay the development of AIDS.

A seronegative result usually indicates that you are not infected with HIV. However, you should be re-tested in six months if you have engaged in high-risk behavior during the past six months because it can take this long for your immune system to produce enough antibodies. During the six months between exposure and the test, it is important to protect yourself and others from possible exposure to HIV.

If your HIV test result is negative, it does not mean your partner is negative also. Your HIV test results reveal only your HIV status. Because HIV is not necessarily transmitted every time there is an exposure, your HIV test does not reveal whether or not your partner is infected. Your partner must be tested also. **HIV testing should never be used in place of protecting yourself from infection.**

Anyone with a sexually transmitted disease (STD) or who has had an STD should get tested for HIV. HIV can easily enter the body through sores caused by STDs like syphilis and herpes. People with HIV infection should tell their sexual and needle-sharing partners to seek counseling and testing.

If you get an HIV test, I strongly recommend that you go back for your results and talk with a qualified HIV/AIDS counselor. The counselor can provide emotional support and help interpret your test results. Counselors can explain treatment options, discuss lifestyle factors that can keep you healthy longer and advise on methods to avoid spreading HIV to others. Counseling can be done in person or over the telephone.

HIV testing may be either confidential or anonymous. Confidential testing means that, while you will have to give your name, the test results are private. They won't be shared with anyone except under special conditions, such as a legal subpoena. With anonymous testing, you do not provide your name. You are given a code to obtain your test results. Testing policies vary from state to state. At the testing site, ask for an explanation of their policies and procedures.

Treatment

There is no cure for HIV infection or AIDS. There is no vaccine against HIV. People with HIV infection can be given several drugs to slow down the attack on their immune (self defense) systems. The drugs are expensive and may cause side effects. Everyone with HIV infection is expected to develop AIDS sooner or later.

Therapies have been developed to fight both HIV infection and its associated infections. The Food and Drug Administration (FDA) have approved a number of drugs for the treatment of HIV infection. The first group of drugs used to treat HIV infection, called *nucleoside analog reverse transcriptase inhibitors* (NRTIs), interrupt an early stage of the virus replication. These drugs may slow the spread of HIV in the body and delay the onset of opportunistic infections. It is important to know that these drugs do not prevent transmission of HIV to other individuals.

Another group of anti-HIV drugs, called *protease inhibitors*, interrupt virus replication at a later step in its life cycle. Because HIV can become resistant to each group of drugs, combination treatment using both is necessary to effectively suppress the virus. These drugs do not cure people of HIV or AIDS, and they all have side effects that can be severe. The most common side effects associated with protease inhibitors include nausea, diarrhea and other gastrointestinal symptoms.

Just to give you a brief understanding of the seriousness of being infected, the attention to details is necessary. Suppose you are infected. Your daily schedule of school and work may interfere with you taking your medications. You might forget how many pills to take, mix up the required combination of pills, or have bouts with depression or emotional challenges that may arise from the pressures. Drugs taken incorrectly can lead to rapid emergence of high-level resistance.

There are also other health concerns that the infected person must attend to, such as, mental health counseling and nutritional counseling and support. You will have to learn how to prepare low or non-fat meals, the kind of diet that is required for certain kinds of medication to be most effective. You will have to be instructed on the risks and benefits of each medicine. You would also have to deal with some of the side-effects of anti-viral drugs you may be required to take.

One major problem for many HIV infected persons is the lack of financial resources to obtain needed medication. If you have difficulty holding a job, other supportive services will have to assist you - food bank, case management, housing, etc., to meet your array of needs.

Adherence Monitoring
The HIV infected person is placed on a treatment regimen. Again, the medicine is either for slowing the spread of the HIV virus or trying to keep the AIDS virus from reproducing. The treatment regimen varies, depending upon the progression of the virus. It is imperative that an infected person take their pills the same time every day. Forgetting to take them can cause problems.

Research findings indicate that missing a single day of combination therapy (pills) can promote the development of resistance. Also, *taking the pills incorrectly can lead to rapid emergence of high level resistance to that medication.* Another treatment regimen has to be introduced.

An adherence monitor makes sure you have the necessary support system and assists you in your treatment regimen. One of the latest services is to supply HIV infected clients with pagers that automatically signal when it is time to take their medication. Monitoring may also require home visits and transportation to take HIV clients to their physician appointments.

Prevention
Since no cure for HIV is available, the only way to prevent infection by the virus is to avoid behaviors that put you at risk of infection, such as sharing needle, unprotected sexual intercourse, and drug use that inhibits your judgment and increases risky behaviors.

Because many people infected with HIV have no symptoms, there is no way of knowing with certainty whether a sexual partner is infected unless he or she has been repeatedly tested for the virus or has not engaged in any risky behavior.

At best, the Centers For Disease Control can only recommend that people either abstain from sexual intercourse or protect themselves by using a latex condom whenever having vaginal, anal or oral sexual intercourse.

It's On You Youngin!
Now that you've been educated on the perils of Booty Call, you

got to decide what you're gonna do with all these playa', stud, mac daddy, _itch, ho, hoochie talkin' people and lifestyles. I'm playa' hatin' on all those musicians, entertainers, actors, (and your so-called friends) who, by their lifestyle, words and behavior, are influencing children and youth to become involved in premarital sexual activity, alcohol and drug use, and all other negativity! Either they are part of your problem or part of your solution! Just 'cause they got some fame, some ice, some bank and a few platinum CDs, don't mean they care about you.

The lyrics, music videos, movies or magazines that hype Booty Call and negativity come with a price that's to high to pay! And certainly, they aren't going to take responsibility for you if you get infected. Are they going to come visit you in the hospital intensive care unit when your body is wracked with AIDS? Please! If you get it, you're on your own. That's how they roll!

But later for them. It's about you and your health. Do you know your HIV status? If you have engaged in unprotected sexual intercourse, you need to be tested! What you don't know can hurt you and a lot of other people! **You don't need a Booty Call, you need to make a "Clinic Call!"**

Chapter Sources
• Dr. Dwayne Nosakhere Thomas
• American Association for World Health
• The National Institute of Allergy and Infectious Diseases
• Bureau of STD Control
• Straight Talk: A Magazine For Teens
• Joint Center for Political and Economic Studies
• The National Institute of Allergy and Infectious Diseases
• Center For Disease Control
• Drugs, Alcohol and Tobacco (Meeks, Heit & Page)
• Deadly Consequences, (Prothrow-Stith & Weissman)
• Center For Disease Control (CDC)

Bling, Bling?

"Beware of covetousness, for a man or woman's life does not consist of the abundance of things that he or she possesses. A certain rich man owned a lot of land, and year after year his farms produced large crops (and his orchards were brimming with fruit). Soon he didn't know where to store them all. He thought to himself, 'What am I going to do with all these crops? Where am I going to store them all?' Then he said, "I know what I'll do! I'll tear down the old barns and build bigger ones, then I'll have plenty of room for my crops. After that I'll retire and take it easy the rest of my life. I will eat, drink and be happy.' But Yahweh said to him, 'Fool, you're going to die tonight, then whose going to own all those things you worked so hard to get?' So it is with those who work to get everything they want for themselves and make no effort to get to know Yahweh's purpose for your life" (Luke 12:15-21).

I want to call this man in the story, Bling. He isn't too much different from many young people who are on a single mission to accumulate as much as they can. The problem is that Bling lost perspective. When you lose perspective, you lose your balance. When you loose your balance...bam! You fall hard.

Yahshua Messiah told this story. He started the story by saying, *"Beware of covetousness, for a man or woman's life does not consist of the abundance of things that he or she possesses."* Whenever you see the word, "Beware," it should make you stop, look and listen. For example, when you see a, "Beware of Dog" sign, don't ignore it. You might get bit! The warning should at least cause you to slow your roll and check it out.

Yahshua Messiah knew that covetousness will cause a person to become aggressively self-centered. Covetousness is the greed of getting instead of giving. A covetous person can't see beyond themselves, until something brings them back to reality, and then they discover what is really important - sometimes it's too late. This is my version of Yahshua Messiah's story:

I want to take you with me up to Bling's estate. As we pull up to the iron gate, we speak our names into an intercom. A red light blinks as the computer is making a security background check on us. The iron gates open and we drive up on Bling's property. Bling is into agriculture. As we pull up in front of Bling's mansion, he comes out, greets us and offers to show us around. We see acres and acres of wheat waving gently at us in the soft summer wind. His orchards are ripe, his trees brimming with fruit. His barns are full. They cannot hold any more grain.

Bling takes us to see his horses. His imported Arabian horses are impressive. Next, Bling shows us his olympic size swimming pool which is in the shape of a dollar $ign. From there, we go to his six car garage. Bling pushes a remote and all six doors slide back simultaneously. There is a Lamborgini, a Benz limo, a Lexus SUV, a vintage 1956 Thunderbird, an Excaliber, and a Stutz Bearcat. (A Stutz costs one hundred thousand dollars and has a solid gold dashboard!)

Next, Bling takes us inside his mansion. As we walk into the vestibule, a stunning crystal chandelier hangs from the ceiling. We go downstairs to his game room. He has Play Station 2, arcade games, cyberspace games, archery, a firing range, the works!

Finally, Bling takes us upstairs to his bedroom. As we walk in, he pushes a button and his sports clothes closet opens. He has the latest sweat suits, Nikes', a basketball autographed by Michael and Magic, and other expensive sports paraphernalia. He pushes another button and his clothier closet opens. He has seven hundred suits with a brand new pair of shoes for each suit. Brooks Bros., Armani, and St. Laurent, were some of his suits.

What tripped us out was Bling's super king-size heart-shaped bed in the center of his room. And in the center of his bed was a marble jacuzzi! You could just take off the padded covering and slide down into the jacuzzi!

Bling had everything, it seemed. Cars, clothes, ice, mansion, a

prosperous business - everything! But Bling wasn't happy. Someone said, **"Happiness is where you find it but rarely where you
seek it!"** So I said, "What's up Bling? Why you lookin' so
gloomy?" Bling said, "Follow me."

We followed Bling downstairs to his office. Bling said, "Look!"
We looked out of his large office window and saw his crops, his
orchards, and his barns. Bling said, "I've got to do something
about that!" "About what?" "My crops and orchards. I don't
have any more room for them!" Then, as if a light came on, Bling
said, "I know what I will do! I'll tear down these barns and build
bigger ones! Then I'll have enough room to store my crops. After
that, I'm gonna just chill, eat, drink and be happy!"

Bling went to his desk. He had the kind of telephone that you
didn't dial, you just said the name into the speaker and it dialed
automatically. "Mr. Jones." In a moment, Mr. Jones answered.
"Mr. Jones, I need you to come to my estate immediately."

While Bling was talking to Mr. Jones, something dawned on me.
Bling never gave Yahweh the glory for shining the sun down on
his crops. Bling never acknowledged Yahweh for showering the
rain down on his orchards. He acted like he pulled it off himself.
Bling never thought about the children in the inner city who live
between a smile and a tear - who go to be hungry most nights.

In twenty minutes, Mr. Jones, an architect, was there and we
quietly followed Bling and Mr. Jones around Bling's estate. Bling
said, "Let's pull down this barn and build it three times larger. I
want this grainery removed, rebuilt larger, and put on the other
side of my estate." On and on Bling talked, as Mr. Jones took
meticulous notes to take back to his office and transcribe into
blueprints. Mr. Jones left. Bling said to us, "Let's eat!" (We were
wondering when we were gonna get our grub on!)

You would not believe Bling's dining room. It looked like a ban-
quet hall! Servants standing at attention on both sides of the
table. Bling sat at the head of the table and we sat down near the
other end of the table. The 12 course meal was all that! Bling fin-
ished eating, pushed away from the table, wiped his mouth with
his silk napkin and burped! And then we heard the voice, "Fool,

you're going to die tonight. Now who's going to get everything you worked your behind off to get?" It was the Creator (Yahweh) speaking to Bling.

The news of his impending death hit Bling like a ton of bricks! I said, "Yo Bling, we gotta jet, man." We didn't know how it was going down, but we weren't going to be around when Bling got took out! As we left, Bling was staring straight ahead in disbelief, shaking like a leaf!

I'm gonna dissect this story and draw parallels with the Hip-Hop generation. When the words, *bling, bling* are mentioned, most adults don't have the slightest ideal what it is, but young people know exactly what bling, bling is. It's all about show. *What you got / What you wearing / The ice, the gold, the Rolex.*

I'm playa' hatin' all ya'll youngins, who like Bling, are totally oblivious to the needs of others, even your mama! She asks you to do something / *But you don't have time / You got to do something else / You get an attitude 'cause she's breakin' into your time. It's all about your self indulgence / It's all about you coming out the store with a new pair.. / with a new shirt / with a new jacket / with a new CD / with bling, bling!* When is the last time you bought your mama something? (I'm not talkin' about birthdays or holidays).

The obsession for money and material acquisition among this Hip-Hop culture is off the hook! In the story, Bling got caught up. So are many of you. But your attention can be gotten. When Yahweh said, *"Bling, you're gonna die tonight,"* what was really valuable and important came into perspective for Bling - *life, health* and *family* - but it was too late!

I watch youngins every day gettin' caught up in money and materialism. Their priorities are all screwed up. They don't realize that longevity is not promised to them, and like Bling, they fail to focus on what is really important. *Most youngins get so caught up in the acquiring the externals (what they are wearing and what they own) that they ignore what needs to be acquired on the inside.*

Bling got shook back to reality by his impending demise. By

nature, humans fear death. Self-preservation is the first law of our being. Most of us will suffer anything or do anything to avoid death. Even though some youngins flirt with death, or prophesy their eventual death like Tupac and Biggie did, or try to act like they're not afraid to die, they don't really want to die.

Catastrophic news has a way of quickly getting our attention. Like Bling, some things you think are important and you can't live without, one day (hopefully sooner than later) you will see them for what they really are - unimportant and insignificant. What would you really rather have, *bling, bling* or good health?

Tragedy has a way of reordering our priorities. It has a way of putting what is really important in life in perspective. If you're not fake, having parents who love and respect you is much more important than having all the latest things. Tommy, Rolex, Nike, Gap, Phat Farm, Timberland, Nextell, ice, whatever, all have to be kept in perspective. Bling lost perspective, his balance, and ultimately his life! Too many youngins are losing perspective too. Some are losing their lives over things. What's going to get your attention and change your perspective and priorities? I don't know. But something will. It's just a matter of time.

Let's go back to what Yahshua Messiah said, *"Beware of covetousness, for a man or woman's life does not consist of the abundance of things that he or she possesses."* To put it another way, **"You are not what you have, but you are what has you."** *You love things and use people when you should love people and use things.* There are too many youngins trying to find their identity in what you have instead of who you are, and what you have been created to be.

A good life does not depend upon the quantity of your possessions, but on the quality of your character. CHARACTER IS THE REAL BLING, BLING! Back in the day, there was a song, "Not on the outside, but inside strong!" It's the character you develop inside that earn people's admiration and respect.

When you are preoccupied with getting external things, you may forget about developing internal qualities that make good character. When you are so obsessed with how you look and what you are wearing, you may neglect to obtain the essential traits for personal growth and development.

Back in the day, I told a honey (who was obsessed with how she looked and what she was wearing), "Your face is your card that gets you into places your intellect wouldn't!" She said, "What do you mean?" I said, "That's just what I mean!" Duh?

You are seriously insecure and immature when you try to get attention by compensating on the outside for what is missing on the inside. You can wear all the ice, the platinum, gold, you want, but if you do not possess essential attributes of character, you're just a designer clothes rack, a shoe tree and a hat rack! Check out this poem I wrote entitled, **"What Is Fresh?"**

*"What is Fresh, some tell me quick, What is fresh? And please don't make me sick! Fresh is a jacket by Phat Farm; Fresh is a Rolex watch to sport on your arm; Fresh is your shades to keep it dark; Fresh is your Navigator to wax in the park; Fresh is your Sean Jean jeans for $75 a pair; Fresh is your dreadlocs to flaunt in your hair; Fresh is your compact disk kickin' gangsta rap; Fresh is steppin' out in your NY Yankee cap. But what is Fresh? Fresh is your Gucci trio - palm pad, brief and clutch; Fresh is your music collection in which you spent so much; Fresh is your greatest dreams of money in the bank; Fresh is the the home you want with a marble jacuzzi tank; Fresh is that large screen DVD with remote control; Fresh is XXX movies where fornication is so bold; Fresh is hoping that one day your name will be in lights; Fresh is your conversation so people with think you are bright; Fresh is smokin' weed, blunt is the name; Fresh is Vince Carter on the court, throwin' down, that's his game! But what is Fresh? After all these things you do, it is a fact that these things don't fully satisfy you? Suppose you were sick and about to die, would you call these Fresh things to your aid? Or maybe your life you're about to lose, would your last request be braids? 211 or blunt won't come to mind, or that tight cell phone you gotta find; **There will be one thought that's deep and broad, is my life right with Yah (God),** now that's Fresh!"*

Now I'm comin' straight - no chaser! What Bling and a lot of youngins are ignoring are two things - *death* and *judgment*. They're coming. And when they go down, you ain't gonna need Versace; you're gonna need a right character! King Solomon gives youngins counsel that should not be ignored:

"Be grateful for every year Yahweh gives you, because no matter how long you live, you will die. Young people, enjoy life while you can. Be happy and let your heart cheer you in your youth, and follow your desires, but remember, everything has its consequences, either good or bad, and Yahweh will one day judge whatever you do" (Ecclesiastes 11:7-9).

Yahweh does not honor what we accumulate. What Yahweh honors is what we genuinely do for people who are in need. Read Matthew 25:31-46 to understand my point. External bling, bling is all about *reputation*. Internal bling, bling is all about *character*.

You can't get instruction in character from BET, MTV, HBO or Def Comedy Jam. You won't develop a righteous character from listening to Death Row or Bad Boy Records. You'll never learn about character from Yo,'Source, or 360.com. They'll tell you themselves that they are not in the business of helping youth develop character. They only hype reputation.

Recognize, reputation is what you fall for, but character is what you stand for. If you don't stand for something, you will fall for anything! One of the greatest needs today is young people with character!

With a right character, you are able to keep life in perspective. You can keep your balance. The desire to impress people with what you have will never put you where you need to be in life. You've got to have substance over style if you expect to reach noble and lofty goals. Furthermore, material acquisition is no indication that you are a successful person. It could just mean you're in a whole lot of debt! It is the building and maintaining of a good character that make you truly successful in life. Sure, it's easier for you to look the part of outward success than it is to actually be truly successful. You can fake on the outside. But you can't fake character because it's an inside job.

Real Bling, Bling Is From The Inside-Out

Character ripens slowly. It takes a while to build a good character, but it can all be torn down with one stupid act, one dumb decision. Character is not an immediate acquisition like purchasing a gold chain. You can't go in a store and pick out character like you can a pair of Nikes. Character development takes time and it takes work. *There are no shortcuts!*

When it comes to male-female relationships, you need someone with character; someone you can *trust*, someone who is *honest* and *responsible*, someone who is *kind* and *patient*, someone who has an *optimistic view* of people and life, someone who has a good *work ethic*. Those are attributes of character. What is on the inside radiates outwardly.

Are you honest and responsible? That means you don't lie, cheat or steal, and you put your home, school and job before hangin' out. *Are you kind and committed?* That means you treat people like you want to be treated and you are dependable. *Do you have an optimistic view of people and life?* That means you think the best of people instead of the worse and you have a positive outlook on life, regardless of life's challenges.

Do you possess a good work ethic? That means you do what needs to be done without being told, and when you are given a task, you will do it right the first time so that you don't have to do it over again. If you can answer yes to each of these questions, then you are on your way toward a noble character.

King Solomon said, *"A good name (character) is better than rubies (bling, bling)."* Solomon also talks about a virtuous woman. He says, *"A virtuous woman is worth more than the costliest jewels"* (Proverbs 31:10-31). **Real Bling, Bling consists of the gold of a good attitude, the diamonds of dignity, and the platinum of patience and peace**.

It is a fact of life that all of nature functions from center-to-circumference - from the inside out, not from the outside-in. It is the ingredients within that makes the outside as valuable as it is. One of the best ways to learn how to develop character is to read the Scriptures. There is a lot of instruction in character development.

Let me say one more thing about acquiring character. **One of the essentials in maintaining a good character is to choose your friends well!** An African proverb says, *"If I really want to know who you are, I must look at your friends."* Your choice of friends will have much to do with you developing character or getting a reputation. It is said that *"birds of a feather flock together."* That's true. You've never seen an eagle and a pigeon kickin' it. Eagles fly high above the fray, while pigeons hang on the corner. You usually assimilate the traits of those you associate with. And, beware of cliques! All I'm saying is, choose your friends well. Good friendships are a priceless commodity. They are rare and need to be preserved.

The 10 Commandments Of Excellence

My wife's brother, Stephen E. Patterson wrote these are solid maxims for developing a well-rounded character:

1) **Promptness**: Time management is crucial in order to complete your goals and to be able to be depended upon. If your goal is to be at work earlier than required it is likely that you will never be late. "Aim High"...if you miss your goal you will still be better then average.

2) **Meeting Deadlines**: Procrastination is often the reason for not meeting your deadline. If there is no deadline set for you, set your own early deadline and stay ahead in your work. Mistakes often happen when people are playing "catch up" or trying to function under pressure.

3) **Pursue Further Education**: You want to become so qualified for your job that you are capable of instructing others. You want to feel not just qualified but certified. It is good to seek continuing education. Don't wait until it becomes necessary or mandatory.

4) **Socializing**: If you are a very sociable person, and that is one

of your gifts, it is not uncommon for one's gift to become their weakness. Be selective of your friends and your socializing at work and away from work. Be careful of allowing friendships to jeopardize your credibility and professionalism. Your work phone is a business phone. Don't start the practice of friends calling you at work for things that can wait until after work.

5) **Financial Management**: Money is important and should be valued and respected. It is good to open a savings account. If you are one who have a desire to help some people, remember, you can't help everyone. Don't allow family or friends to make you feel guilty if it is not wise to meet their request. The economy of this country flip-flops. We know not what tomorrow will bring. Think and plan for the future. Clothing is important but don't become wasteful and addicted to having to buy something new every pay period.

6) **Personal Male/Female Relationships**: You deserve to be complimented, not compromised. You deserve serious love, not deceptive lust. You deserve quality friendship, not a selfish relationship. There are four kinds of people out there: a) *Those who add to you* b) *Those who subtract from you* c) *Those who multiply you* d) *Those who divide you.*

Of course, you are not to be subtracted and divided. A relationship should add to you or multiply you. Be sure you have a spiritual criteria for your selection and allow patience to have a prominent place in your life. Life is too precious to have your beauty and gifts subtracted and are loyalties and focus divided. Your wedding should be the crowning act of beauty and security.

7. **Spiritual Development**: The principles of Yahshua Messiah (Christ), the values of the Word of God, the natural beauty of righteous living, the presence that comes from a joyful heart, the classy feeling you experience when God makes you feel good about yourself, are so important to the attaining of your goals, that you dare not live without this kind of security. Regular

church attendance keeps your mind focused. Daily devotion in God's word and spiritual books keeps you enlightened and strong. Obedience to what you know is right makes you feel good. Praying at least three times a day keeps the presence of God with you. Talking about God's goodness makes you His witness. Decide that your spiritual development is a priority.

8. **Visualization** is important to keep your dreams and goals fresh. Think about what you want to achieve. Pray about those things and God will give you a mental, colorful photograph of your desire. The mental photograph keeps you motivated and determined to press through any obstacle that may arise. *Don't expose your 16x40 dream to 5x7 mentalities around you.* Seek other dreamers and achievers as your friends and let others be mere associates.

9. **Creating A Positive Image Of Yourself At Work**: The image you create will have a lot to do with the success you experience at your job. Perceptions are powerful and can work for you or against you. Some of the things that create an image of you are: Style, i.e., dress, deportment and decorum, personality, i.e., attitude, communication (what you say and how you say it).

10. **Producing Excellent Work**: The lack of available jobs and the spirit of competition admonishes us to strive to be the best in our field and produce quality work. It's important to read pertinent material, to possess the aids and reference books that add to your knowledge, to attend seminars and to use and value mentors in your field. *Never take your position for granted or feel that you are indispensable. You are not indispensable and you should produce the calibre of work that will make it hard to replace you.*

Scrubs and Pigeons?

"How can they hit us and still be our heroes? How can they hit us and still be our leaders? Our husbands? Our lovers? Our geniuses? Our friends? They can't, can they?"
- Pearl Cleage, Author and Activist

I'm playa' hatin' again! Scrubs and Pigeons ain't nothin' but a hanky-head continuum of African American males and females being pimped by the corporate-controlled music industry to diss each other! I'm playa' hatin' because these confused youngins show they have no knowledge of the historical context in which these denigrating characterizations are rooted, and because they don't know the history, they are repeating it!

The historical context of African males and females putting each other down is largely rooted in a complex set of circumstances. Divide-and-conquer has historically been part and parcel of white supremacy global domination.

The flagrant disregard for male-female relationships during the European enslavement of Africans fostered a physical and eventually, a psychological rift, that continues to impact daily on the lives and relationships of African American males and females.

Historical Context

• *Marriage among enslaved Africans was not recognized or protected by law. The slave holder would often choose husbands for the women and wives for the men. Often the slave holder would mate the husband and wife for breeding purposes. The husband could see his wife only if the slave holder saw fit.*

• *Enslaved husbands and wives were purposely separated and sent to different plantations. Slave holders did not care about stable relationships among African males and females, which led to a systematic destabilization of the African family and home.*

• *The slave holder fostered unequal treatment between field slaves and house slaves causing dissension and hostility among slaves.*

• *Enslaved males and females were greatly prohibited from making the kinds of physical and emotional bonding that lent to healthy, wholesome male-female relationships.*

The other phenomenon that was given birth out of the enslavement of African males and females was a redefinition of African humanity. The redefinition was largely accomplished through **denigrating images** and **negative identification**.

Denigrating Images

"The roots of the schism (division) go back to slavery. Both the popular theater and the literature of the antebellum period created standardized images of slaves and their masters. These initial representations were used to rationalize the enslavement of African people and to justify the institution of slavery in the South."

As early as 1781, a black character named Sambo appeared on the American stage. Hear the insight of the historian Joseph Boskin: *"Sambo was an extraordinary type of social control, at once extremely subtle, devious and encompassing. To exercise a high degree of control meant also to be able to manipulate the full range of humor, to create ultimately, an insidious type of buffoon. To make the black male into an object of laughter, and conversely, to force him to devise laughter, was to strip him of his masculinity, dignity and self respect. Sambo was, then, an illustration of humor as a device of oppression and one of the most potent [characters] in American popular culture. **The ultimate objective for whites was to effect mastery, to render the black male powerless as a potential warrior, as a sexual competitor, as an economic adversary.**"*

William Van Deburg observed: *"The early slave image offered white audiences a comforting psychological reassurance...such intellectually inferior clowns posed little threat to white hegemony (authority)."*

Most Southern writers in the postbellum era brought new black stereotypes. The denigrating female image became the domestic, docile mammy caricature - Aunt Jemima - while the male side evolved into an elderly, submissive, hat-in-hand Negro.

Negative Identification

A successful ploy by slave holders is to control the language. When oppressors control the language they can redefine those whom they oppress. Negative identification like n-----r, coon, pickaninny, burr head, and other derogatory and divisive terminology became the common language used by whites against Africans in America. The corporate controlled media is largely responsible for keeping negative labels fresh in the collective psyche of mainstream America. (But it is the corporate-controlled music industry that is exacerbating the friction between brothas and sistas - the *scrub* and *pigeon* scenario.)

The success of negative identification is two-fold: a) the negative labels are generally believed by mainstream America as true toward whom they are directed b) those to whom negative labeling is directed oftentimes assimilate them unconsciously. *When an individual/group assimilate negative identification, it usually becomes a self-fulfilling prophecy!* It shows in their behavior.

Consequently, it becomes nearly impossible for white America to purge these negative images and labels from their thought processes, and it is difficult for the people of color who have assimilated negative identification to overcome the societal stigmatism and the subsequent behaviors. Case in point - *If you call yourselves doggs, doggs will act like doggs!*

I'm playa' hatin' the brothas who call each other "dogg!" "Was' up dogg?" "Where my doggs at?" And then brothas got the nerve to bark like a real dog! Please! How have brothas gone from African kings to doggs? Don't call me dogg! I don't answer to it! I ain't nobody's dogg - never was, never will be!

I'm playa' hatin' when brothers call females b-----s, ho's and hoochies. After all African American women have suffered and continue to suffer in this country and then to be called these disrespectful and degrading names by brothas is inexcusable and indefensible!

I'm playa' hatin' the sistas who use the words n----r and b----! We got sistas callin' brothers scrubs, faggots and a plethora of denigrating names - and gettin' paid by oppressors to do it! After all African American men have suffered and continue to suffer in this country and then to be called these disrespectful and demeaning names by the sistas is equally inexcusable and indefensible!

So many youngins don't understanding *Nommo* - the power of *the Word*. Words create. What is being created by the negative side of Hip-Hop culture with these confrontational words is a climate between brothas and sistas that is reaping grave consequences in male-female relationships.

Verbal Put-downs and Its Consequences

The corporate-controlled media instigated and encouraged verbal put-downs between African American males and females. Back in the day, popular sitcoms such as, *Sanford and Son* had Fred Sanford and Aunt Esther dissin' each other. On the *Jeffersons*, it was George Jefferson and Florence the maid puttin' each other down. On *Good Times*, J.J and his sister Thelma went at it verbally like cats and dogs!

While they were dissin' each other, in the guise of comedy, a subliminal seduction was at work in the collective psyche of African American people. We began to accept put-downs as normal. While we were laughin' and gettin' played, corporate advertisers were givin' us the finger and gettin' paid!

The negative side of Hip-Hop culture has taken put-downs between African American males and females to another level. *The strong African images and examples of manhood and womanhood of the Yoruba, Ashanti, Mandingo, and the Maroons in the Caribbean, are passe' and replaced with dogg, hoochie, playa', mac daddy, ho, G, thug, scrub and pigeon!*

Deeper still, there are disturbing consequences for the verbal put-downs that go on between African American males and females. It puts pressure on males and females and creates artificial standards for acceptance/behavior. Here is a partial listing:

- Physical features become a primary criteria for acceptance or rejection by the opposite sex
- Character is less important than physical features, selfish interests and materialism
- Serious and substantive communication is inhibited
- Understanding and appreciation for the opposite sex is limited
- Blatant disrespect for one another is fostered
- Exploits the deficiencies of opposite sex: No car, money, unkempt hair or nails, no latest clothes/styles
- Confrontational communication. Telling each other off
- Comparing to males or females outside their relationship
- A challenge to one's manhood or womanhood
- Venting frustrations on each other may lead to regretful actions and consequences

Disrespect and verbal put-downs between males and females can be dangerous. Domestic conflicts and violence while dating is increasing in African American male-female relationships, even among young couples. According to the authors of the book, Cool Pose: The Dilemmas of Black Manhood in America, there is danger in male-female put-downs.

"Male-female conflict may develop when a female criticizes her partner for his inability to support the family. Or when she raises her voice (even worse if it is "around the guys"). He takes this as further insult to an already jeopardized sense of manhood and self-esteem, and may become violent to save face. Many black men feel that, even though they may not be able to control how society treats them, at the very least they should be able to control "their woman."

Check out how ridiculous this woman sounds: This is what Shahrazad Ali says in her book, The Blackman's Guide To Understanding The Black Woman: *"When she (the black woman) crosses this line and becomes viciously insulting it is time for the Blackman to soundly slap her in the mouth. She may also have to be physically restrained until her anger and shock passes. It's okay to restrain her, she won't burst and no Blackwoman can win a physical fight against a right Blackman...Soon she will become trained to curb her vicious tongue when talking to him...She'll cry and scream and scratch like a wild animal...and she must be dealt with as such."*

This next quotation is an excerpt from Time Magazine, September 3, 1990. This is Ike Turner being quoted. Ike used to be married to the singer, Tina Turner.

"After the first show, I changed clothes, and on my way out, Tina was standing close to the door and she screamed at me," Ike recalls. *"I said, 'Don't talk to me like that,' and it was just WHACK!"* He claps his hands hard for emphasis. *"I wasn't even thinking, because she was screaming, and I can't stand for a woman to scream at me, man, I swear to God, man."*

When it was time for the next performance, he says, *"She came on stage -- she's a strong woman, man -- she did the whole show. Afterwards, I said, 'Where you wanna eat?' She said, 'Ike, take me to the hospital. I think my jaw is broke!' She did the whole show without me being able to detect it!"*

The African American author and activist, Pearl Cleage inquires: *"So the question is: How can they hit us and still be our heroes? How can they hit us and still be our leaders? Our husbands? Our lovers? Our geniuses? Our friends? They can't. Can they?"*

To be sure, domestic violence works both ways. There are females who have committed atrocities against their boyfriends and husbands or their property. One famous entertainer got hot grits poured on his back by a woman while he was in the bath tub! It was reported that a famous young woman, (whose music group is the inspiration for this chapter) burned her boyfriend's house down! A popular movie showed a jilted woman torching her man's car! And who can forget the man who got his penis cut off by his wife who claimed she retaliated because of his verbal and physical abuse. Ouch!

Even though the songs that refer to some brothas as "scrubs" and some sistas as "pigeons" is old, I am simply using them to represent the continuum of a long and painful train of negative labels and verbal put-downs between African American males and females in which too many African American musicians, comedians and entertainers are being purchased to put down their own people.

The widespread acceptance and use of put-downs in Hip-Hop culture, and the blatant disrespect for the opposite sex become a precursor for violent or abusive relationships - verbal and physical. A lot of young males going upside their honey's head! And there females who are getting whacked and fighting back!

Although verbal and physical abuse is a two-way street, statistics overwhelmingly show males to be more physically abusive. The following warning signals may indicate trouble for a female (or a male) in need of professional intervention, such as, counseling, conflict resolution skills, or anger management to resolve abusive tendencies.

Warning Signals For Women: Anticipating Violence Or An Abusive Relationship
1. Shouting, hollering, excessive cursing, name calling, sarcasm
2. Finger pointing or fist waving, especially in and around your face
3. Arm or wrist grabbing or twisting
4. Throwing or breaking things
5. Hitting his hand or fist against walls, tables, steering wheel, etc., or reckless fast driving
6. Threatening to do violent things to himself, you, your family, your friends, your children
7. Indicating that he has a gun or other weapon
8. Bringing up past arguments or wrongdoing for which he holds you responsible
9. Following you, spying on you, questioning you about your whereabouts or your friends, male or female
10. Locking doors so you are trapped in a care or house and you can't leave whenever you want to leave

Now that you have a better understanding of the historical context, as well as the unfortunate consequences that may result from assimilating negative labels and verbal put-downs, knowledge is limited without direct action. Individually, we must stop putting each other down. Collectively, we need to boycott the perpetrators of negativity. This may sound ambitious, but we can bring about change. *I'm not suggesting censorship, but I am suggesting using our good sense to choose not to purchase or support any movies, videos, music, project or person that demean, degrade and denigrate African American females, males, children, families and our communities.*

It's long overdue that we hold the corporate-controlled music industry responsible, and the musicians and entertainers accountable for disrespecting us! We need to hit them where it hurts - right below the belt - in the wallet and pocketbook! Why should we pay to be dissed and denigrated? I'm not!

The "divide and conquer" game has gone on long enough! Africans in America have been forced, (and now paid) to be the main playas' in the game. If we are to have wholesome male-female relationships, we are going to have to stop doing those things that are creating our problems and start doing the things that will bring solutions.

You Can't Be What You Can't See

Most of the popular brothas and sistas who youngins try to imitate in dress, lifestyle and behavior, are not men or women, just males and females. All men are males, but not all males are men. All women are females, but not all females are women.

Buffed or phat bodies don't make them a man or woman! Manhood and womanhood is a maturation process that includes physical, mental-emotional, spiritual, social and cultural growth and development. This lack of development among many youngins is because they can't be what they can't see! They're looking in all the wrong places!

Today, many youngins are *influenced* when they should be *developed.* When you let someone influence you, you will imitate and fake. When you permit someone to assist you in your development, you will grow and mature.

Edward S. Lathan, a brother who I have had the privilege of interacting with a few times, gave me an insightful booklet he wrote entitled, *"From The Eyes Of A Ladies' Man."* Brother Lathan said, **"To be a man, you must first be able to recognize one."** The same advice goes for females: **"To be a woman, you must first be able to recognize one."**

If you want to be a man, you have to recognize a man, talk to a man, and learn from a man. If you want to be a woman, you have to recognize a woman, talk to a woman, and learn from a woman.

Brother Lathan says: **"When you are ready, your teacher will appear."** He's referring to teachers in the school of life. When you are ready to learn how to be a man or woman - not a thug, not a golddigga, not fake - then a man or woman will appear to teach you. *That means, your eyes will be open to recognize your teacher and you will make yourself available for them to teach you, mentor you and develop you.* We have stable men and women in the "village" able to teach you, when you're ready.

You cannot attain manhood or womanhood on your own. There are no self-made men or women. There must be someone to *take time with you / love you / support you / encourage you / teach you / correct you / challenge you / respect and guide you /* to manhood and womanhood. But you have to put yourself in a position to receive the wisdom, knowledge and skills.

There are no scrubs, pigeons, _itches, doggs or hoochies. Only males and females in need of becoming men and women. Who is your teacher?

Chapter Sources
Split Image: African Americans In The Mass Media
Cool Pose: The Dilemmas Of Black Manhood In America
The Blackman's Guide To Understanding The Black Woman
People Magazine
Mad At Miles
From The Eyes Of A Ladies' Man

The Blunt Truth!

"I thought I'd take a trip just to get away for a while, cut my hair, smoked pot, did a pill or two in an effort to change my style. I tried in every way to please, but I was pleasing everybody but me. Nothing I did, nothing I said was really me. I have to be real, I have to feel what right for me. And what I thought was insecurity was a need in me to be myself. I GOT TO BE MYSELF!" — Voices of East Harlem

Drug use is a huge part of the negative side of Hip Hop culture. To be honest, Hip-Hop got it legitimately. You can't watch a television show without a corporate drug dealer trying to sell you drugs during commercials. America is the biggest drug pusher in the world! Drug and alcohol use is as American as violence!

But guess what? I ain't tryin' to change America. I'm tryin' to change your thinking and behavior, if you're getting high. That's why I'm playa' hatin' the use of drugs and alcohol in Hip-Hop culture! I'm playa' hatin' every drug dealer, whether you're selling dime bags of weed, hustlin' crack or moving kilos. I'm also playa' hatin' those alcohol sellin' ghetto corner stores and those drive-in owners of ghetto liquor stores that keep our young geniuses and future leaders inebriated 24-7. They are the real haters on our youngins and communities!

I'm playa' hatin' all ya'll - "211" and gin drinking / blunt and beedie smokin'/ heroin shootin' and crack tokin' / narcotics sellin' youngins! **The blunt truth is that we are losing some of the best and brightest minds in the African American community to drug and alcohol addiction!** I'm not done yet! I got one more.

"Wasss' uuuup?" What's up is that brothas are sellin' out our people by frontin' alcohol for tha man! Yeah, I'm playa' hatin'! Alcohol has only one purpose - to get you high or drunk - but it has many consequences - some deadly! Sclerosis of the liver,

alcoholism, people killed by drunk drivers, impaired judgment, and a host of other life and family-destroying results! Brothas don't get it. Or maybe they do. They gettin' paid! *The blunt truth is that some of our people can be bought and sold by oppressors that are detrimental to our individual and collective health and well-being!* Everybody from our community is not necessarily for our community!

A clean-cut college graduate brotha sellin' alcohol on a commercial or an African American-owned magazine advertising alcohol is just as dangerous to the African American community's health as a drug dealer on the corner sellin' heroin and crack! What's the difference? Legal versus illegal? Sophisticated versus thug? Please! Drugs and alcohol are substances that destroy lives and wreck families! The next time you see brothas on t.v. saying, "Wasss' uuuup," recognize that they've been purchased!

The next time you see a slick African American-owned magazine that talks about uplifting our people on one page and a liquor advertisement on the next page, recognize hypocrisy! And the next time you hear an alcohol advertisement on a Hip-Hop radio station, recognize that advertisement dollars, not African people, are their number one concern! *That's the blunt truth!*

Drug Misuse and Abuse

Drugs are substances that change the way the body and/or mind work. *Drug misuse is the incorrect use of a prescription or over-the-counter drug.* For example, a doctor might prescribe a painkiller when a person is injured. In this case, the painkiller is used for medical reasons. However, another person might obtain the painkiller illegally and use it for reasons other than pain. This is drug misuse.

Drug abuse is the use of drugs that lessen the user's ability to function normally or that are harmful to the user and others. For example, youth who drink alcohol are involved in drug abuse. Not only is it illegal for them to drink alcohol, but also they do not function normally when drinking alcohol. They are at risk of harming themselves and others when they have been drinking.

The misuse or abuse of alcohol and/or other drugs is a risk factor for being involved in harmful, criminal and/or violent relationships. Harmful relationships are relationships that destroy self-respect, interfere with productivity and health, and include addictions and/or violence.

Drugs That Influence Behavior and Relationships

Sedative-hypnotic drugs: These are drugs that depress the central nervous system and are called "downers." Barbiturates and tranquilizers are examples. Downers are second to alcohol in contributing to harmful and violent behavior.

PCP: Also called, "angel dust," is a drug that changes the way people see things. People who use PCP might have memory and speech problems. They might have bad hallucinations and depression. PCP can cause very violent behavior.

Cocaine: This drug stimulates the central nervous system and its use frequently results in drug dependence. Drug dependence is the continued use of a drug even though it harms the body, mind, and relationships. Cocaine use changes personality in different ways. Some people become very hostile toward others. Other people get very depressed. Cocaine use might result in harming others or in suicide.

Crack: This is a drug that is pure cocaine and produces rapid ups and downs. People who use crack get a very quick "high" that is followed by a rapid drop to "low." People can become dependent on crack immediately. They then will have an urge to get more. They might harm others in order to get the money to pay for the drug. Some turn to giving all kinds of sexual favors just to get crack.

Amphetamines: These drugs "speed up" the central nervous system. This is why they are called "speed." People who use "speed" might become overactive, impulsive, and out of control. When they stop using "speed" they may get very depressed.

Heroin: Heroin slows body functions such as heart rate and breathing and produces drowsiness and mood swings. People who use heroin can become dependent on the drug. Heroin use increases violent behavior. Because heroin is mainly injected into a vein, users who share needles are at risk for HIV infection.

Anabolic steroids: These drugs are produced from male sex hormones. People who use them can experience outbursts of very angry behavior. After prolonged use, depression might occur, putting the user at risk for suicide. Steroids have also been known to cause liver, bladder and pancreas problems.

Marijuana: Also known as "reefer" or "weed." (I'm gonna spend a little more time with weed. This is a gateway drug that usually leads to more addictive drug use. Weed is also Hip-Hop culture's main drug of choice.)

Marijuana (weed) has often been studied in isolation from other drugs. The primary psychoactive ingredient is *delta-9tetrahydrocannabinol* (THC). THC is only one of several hundred ingredients in marijuana smoke, and the smoke contains several dozen additional chemical compounds that are unique to marijuana.

The smoke from weed shares many characteristics with tobacco smoke and presents similar dangers. A comparison of the tars from weed and cigarettes has shown that when smoked the same way, weed produces more than twice as much tar as a popular brand of cigarettes and when inhaled deeply and exhaled slowly, as is usual in smoking weed, it yields nearly four times more tar. These tars cause abnormalities in the lungs such as, inflammation, chronic asthma, bronchitis, emphysema, and possible lung cancer may result from smoking weed.

Weed interferes with complex mental functioning. Smoking weed seems to produce persistent changes in brain function and behavior, such as memory lapses, disorientation, mood changes, and loss of motivation. Weed may cause hallucinations, or cause you to feel threatened and paranoid around others.

Marijuana and Sexuality
Weed has often been said by some users as having aphrodisiac (arousing sexual desire) effects. A substantial proportion of males who smoke weed have had difficulty achieving erections. Long-

term, high dosage use leads to a suppression of the testes and sub-sequent decreased testosterone (the primary male hormone) pro-duction. Male use is also associated with reduced sperm produc-tion, abnormal sperm structure, and impaired sperm mobility. There have even been studies where sterility in males has result-ed from smoking weed. Most of these effects are believed to be reversible when a male stops smoking weed permanently.

Females who smoke weed may experience vaginal dryness, which may account for painful intercourse. There is also some evidence that weed may cause abnormal menstruation, including failure to ovulate. A weed-smoking pregnant female puts her baby in danger. Like cigarettes, smoking weed increases carbon monoxide levels in the mother's blood. This reduces oxygen availability to the fetus. Low birth weight, spontaneous abortion and stillbirths have been linked to mothers smoking weed.

Marijuana is rapidly transmitted into breast milk and remains there for a prolonged period. Although its effects on infants are unknown, breast-feeding is not recommended for mothers who smoke weed and are unwilling to stop.

WARNING: The affect that all these drugs and others have on your judgment and behavior can cause you to be at risk for HIV infection.

More Blunt Truth About Drugs and Relationships

Drugs and relationships are a bad mix. Drug and alcohol use, misuse and abuse interfere with one's judgment and behavior. When you date someone who is under the influence, you are at risk to be misused and abused. It can also escalate into a violent relationship. The following lists the risks you take when drinking or using drugs:

• You might not stick to your decision to practice abstinence
• You increase your risk of getting pregnant or getting some one pregnant
• You increase the risk of becoming infected with HIV and other STDs

- You increase the risk of being in situations in which rape occurs
- Hanging around teens who use drugs put you at risk for having someone put a drug into your food or beverage without your knowledge
- You might become drug dependent and exchange sex for drugs or for money to buy drugs
- You might share a needle that has infected blood on it

Violent Relationships
Violent relationships are relationships that harm another person physically, mentally and/or emotionally. The following are inappropriate behaviors that may result from the use, misuse and abuse of drugs and alcohol.
- *Physical abuse* is harmful treatment that results in physical injury to the victim. Examples include hitting, slapping, kicking, choking, shoving, and other physically harmful behaviors. Physical abuse is also associated with intentional acts of burning, bruising, cutting, shooting, or breaking bones.
- *Emotional abuse* is "putting down" another person and making the person feel worthless. This includes the harmful treatment of a person that is expressed through threats, intimidation, humiliation, blame or degrading. Emotional abuse might be experienced in less obvious ways that are difficult to recognize. An example of more subtle emotional abuse would be teasing that might seem to be humorous but actually is ridicule.
- *Sexual abuse* is sexual contact that is forced on a person. Sexual abuse is expressed in different forms such as, incest, inappropriate touching of private body parts, or the display or production of pornographic pictures.
- *Rape* is the threatened or actual use of physical force to get someone to have sexual intercourse without giving consent. Although rape most commonly is perpetuated by males against females, males are increasingly becoming rape victims of other males and sometimes of females. In nearly three-fourths of the cases, rape is associated with drinking alcohol.

A common perception is that rape is committed by an unknown person. However, the majority of cases of rape involve a form of rape known as acquaintance (date) rape. Acquaintance rape is a rape in which the rapist is known to the person who is raped. Acquaintance rapes often occur in dating situations.

"Roofies" is the nickname for the date rape drug. The clinical name is Flunitrazepam or Rohypnol. It is an odorless, colorless sedative drug. Roofies have effects similar to Valium, but is approximately 10 times more potent. The drug is associated with impaired judgment and impaired motor skills and can make a victim unable to resist a sexual attack.

It is referred to as the "date-rape" drug because it can cause a blackout with complete or partial loss of memory. A male can slip a "roofie" into a female's drink and commit rape after she blacks out. A male who has a drink laced with roofies may be sexually assaulted by other males after he blacks out. It is also known that the drug *Ecstasy* enhances sexual desire and produces an urge to suck resulting in many young girls having unprotected oral sexual activity.

Some males misinterpret actions such as cuddling and kissing as indicating a desire to engage in sexual intercourse. As a result, some males may ignore messages of nonconsent and proceed to engage in sexual activity especially if little verbal physical resistance is encountered. Unfortunately, in sexual abuse, rape, and unprotected sexual activity, HIV or other STDs may be transmitted.

What To Do With A Potential Rapist

(Someone e-mailed this information to me. It could save your life.) *A man who taught a self-defense class has a female friend who was attacked last year in the parking garage one night after work and taken to an abandoned house and raped. The man who taught self-defense started a women's group and began teaching these classes soon after. He is a black belt in karate and trains twice a year with Steven Segall. He and the others in this group interviewed some rapists and date rapists in prison on what they*

look for and here's some interesting facts:
• The number one thing rapists look for in a potential victim is hair style. They are most likely to go after a woman with a pony-tail, bun, braid or other hair style that can easily be grabbed. They are also likely to go after a woman with long hair. Women with short hair are not common targets, but some been raped.
• The second thing rapists look for is clothing. They will look for women who's clothing is easy to remove quickly. The number one outfit they look for is overalls because many of them carry scissors around to cut clothing, and on overalls the straps can be easily cut.
• Rapist also look for women on their cell phone, searching through their purse or doing other activities while walking because they are off guard and can be easily overpowered.
• The time of day men are most likely to attack and rape a woman is in the early morning, between 5 and 8:30 a.m. The number one place women are abducted from or attacked at is grocery store parking lots. Number two is office parking lots or garages. Number three is public restrooms.
• The thing about rapist is that they are looking to grab a woman and quickly move her to a second location where they don't have to worry about getting caught.
• Only 2% said they carried weapons because rape carries a 3-5 year sentence but rape with a weapon is 15-20 years.
• If you put up any kind of a fight at all, they get discouraged because it only takes a minute or two for them to realize that going after you isn't worth it because it will be time-consuming. These convicted rapist said they will not pick on women who have umbrellas in their hands, or other similar objects that can be used from a distance. Keys are not a deterrent because you have to get really close to the attacker to use them as a weapon. So, the idea is to convince these guys you're not worth it.

Defense Tactics To Use Against Potential Rapists
• If someone is following behind you on a street or in a garage or with you in an elevator or stairwell, look them in the face and ask

them a question, like what time is it, or make general small talk. For example, "I can't believe it is so cold out here, we're in for a bad winter." Now you've seen their face and could identify them in a lineup, therefore you lose appeal as a target.

• If someone is coming toward you, hold out your hands in front of you and yell, "Stop or stay back!" Most of the rapists this man talked to said they'd leave a woman alone if she yelled or showed that she would not be afraid to fight back. Again, they are looking for an EASY target.

• If you carry pepper spray (this instructor was a huge advocate of it and carries it with him wherever he goes,) yelling. "I have pepper spray," and holding it out will be a deterrent.

• If someone grabs you, you can't beat them with strength but you can by outsmarting them. If they grab your wrist, pull your wrist back so your hand is in waving position (palm facing forward) and twist it toward yourself and pull your arm away. It is hard to hold onto wrist bones that are moving in that way. They stumble toward you and you stumble back, so you can use that momentum to bring the same out and backhand them with your knuckles in the forehead, nose or teeth.

• If you are grabbed around the waist from behind, pinch the attacker either under the arm between the elbow and armpit or in the upper inner thigh - HARD! One woman in a class this guy taught told him she used the underarm pinch on a guy who was trying to date rape her and was so upset she broke through the skin and tore out muscle strands. The guy needed stitches. Try pinching yourself in those places as hard as you can stand it; it hurts!

• After the initial hit, always go for the groin. Slap or grab and squeeze the guy's testicles as hard as you can! Don't be afraid - your life may be at stake! It is extremely painful. You might think that you'll make him want to hurt you more, but the thing these rapists told the instructor is that they want a woman who will not cause a lot of trouble. Start causing trouble, and he's out of there.

• When the guy puts his hands up to you, grab his first two fingers and bend them back as far as possible with as much pressure pushing down on them as possible.

• Always be aware of your surroundings, take someone with you if you can and if you see any odd behavior, don't dismiss it, go with your instincts. You may feel a little silly at the time, but you'd feel much worse if the guy really was trouble. It's simple stuff that could save your life.

Don't Blunt Your Future

Young brothas, runnin' trains and date rape ain't worth the consequences! But if you are high, it can affect your judgment and you may try something with a honey that you may forever regret! Don't blunt your future trying to be a mac. It might back up on you! Respect the sistas. And "no" means "no!"

As it concerns the law, a person who is under the influence of alcohol or other drugs cannot give legal consent to have sexual intercourse, therefore it can be considered rape, even if the victim did not say, "No." Also, drunkenness or being high on drugs is not a legal defense against date rape. In other words, if a male has been drinking or using drugs before he commits a rape, this is no legal excuse. He is still charged with rape. There are so many youngins incarcerated who can bear witness to what drugs and alcohol can do to your future.

I give props to all you youngins who never used drugs and alcohol. It takes strength to be clean. I also give props to you youngins who have stopped smoking weed and drinking. For whatever reason, it's all good. Now your system can get cleaned out and hopefully, future health problems won't result. I want to caution you youngins who are presently indulging in drugs, alcohol or selling drugs. **The blunt truth is that drugs and alcohol will take you farther than you want to go and keep you longer than you planned to stay!** Don't blunt your future!

Love is the greatest motivator to live clean. Love for our Creator, love for yourself and love for those who love you. It hurts people who love you to have to come to visit you while you are locked down. It hurts people who love you to see you standing on the corner sellin' drugs as they drive by. It hurts loved ones to know that you are sellin' your body for some crack (*crack ho'* is the street term). It hurts the African American community to see you waste so much potential and promise because of an addiction.

   The blunt truth is that the most abused substance is human relationships. Instead of abusing your relationships with those who love you, enhance it by loving yourself and them enough to live clean. If love does not motivate you to live clean, consequences might have to do it. That's the blunt truth!

Chapter Resources
Sexuality & Character Education K-12

Keepin' What Real?

"If you are not your own reality, then whose myth are you?"
- Sun Ra, African American musician, poet, philosopher

Youngin comes to my mind, clear as crystal. He and his four so-called "G's" were on the Montel Williams show. To play on the audience's emotions, Montel was trying to get them to divulge all the crimes they had committed and why? I'll never forget what Youngin said: "WE GOTTA REPRESENT!" That's all he said.

As easy as breathing, these youngins could commit crimes and atrocities of indescribable proportion (in their own community) and all Youngin could say was, "We gotta represent!"

Montel unleashed the audience on them. I didn't like how Montel let it go down. They spewed all kind of invective and condemnation at these youngins on stage. They sat there unphased. When the show was over, Montel hadn't helped these misguided brothas. He only got some ratings that day. That's all his producers probably wanted. Whatever. The four youngins only got a flight to the east coast, a hotel room and forty minutes of disgraceful national exposure! They swore they were *"keepin' it real!"* **Keepin' what real?**

The majority of crimes that go on in African American communities are committed by African Americans. It's our youngins (and some oldheads) who are selling drugs, robbing people, breaking into houses and stores, stealing cars, assaulting and killing people! Every day, senseless, unnecessary crimes are causing untold pain and suffering, mostly in our urban communities, and some youngins got the audacity to boast about it before a national audience! Please! I'm not keepin' the wrongs going on in our communities on the down-low! Call me a playa' hater!

Without a doubt, the American system is whack and perpetrates wrong against people of color, and every incident of injustice must be challenged! But just as we must demand accountability of those outside of our communities, we must also demand accountability from those within our communities. You youngins know right from wrong, and there is no excuse - period!

And then some youngins want to grab a mic and rap about / *growing up in the 'hood' / how hard it is / the poverty / the crime / the violence.* Well, guess who's making it harder with all the crimes being committed? Duh? In case you never knew, I'll tell you how the 'hood' became the 'hood.' **Whenever you take the 'neighbor' off, all you have left is the 'hood!'**

Back in the day, when I was growing up, African Americans may not have had much, but at least we were closer as families , as churches and communities. *We had neighborhoods.* You could leave your door unlocked and come back and nothing was taken. The elders in the community looked out for the children and youth, and if they saw you doing wrong, they could reprimand you. Then they would tell your mama or daddy when they got home! There would be a lot less crime and violence if the 'neighbor' was put back in the 'hood.' (I miss those good ole days, but let me get back to what I was talking about).

I'm not lettin' the system off, but neither am I lettin' youngins who are destroying themselves, each other, and our communities off either! That junk ain't keepin' it real! *It's keepin' inner city our communities crawling with police / it's keepin' the elders scared to go outside / it's keepin' children and youth ducking when they hear gunfire / it's keepin ambulances racing through our streets / and it's keepin' oldheads doing more jury duty than overtime at work!*

Picture this: **During the Million Man March, it was reported that crime was at its lowest ever in the inner cities across America.** In fact, crime that day was reported to be nearly nonexistent. Why? 'Cause brothas was workin' it out! Brothas dropped the thuggin' and fakin' and came together in spirit of Umoja! Brothas made history that day and the whole world saw it! We can be at peace when the thuggin' and fakin' cease. So I'm not down with that "keepin' it real" tip when some of these youngins are part of the problem!

I'm gonna tell you what some youngins have been keepin' real. I'm not broad brushing all youngins, because all youngins are not part of the problem, so if the shoe doesn't fit, cool. I am only citing examples that I observe from some youngins.

Keepin' It Real Ghetto

Understand what "ghetto" is. *Ghetto is not a location, ghetto is a state of mind.* Ghetto is a state of mind that results in behavior that does not uplift or enhance oneself, family and community. Here's an example of ghetto. I was in a grocery store and a young sista was working the cash register. The line was long because her attention was being diverted by a youngin (who was also an employee because he had on the store apron). Youngin walked up to her, talking loud and saying, "I wanna be yo nex baby fava!" "Can I be yo nex baby fava?" He kept saying it over and over. "Can I be yo nex baby fava?" I was trippin'! Now instead of the young sista ignoring him, or quickly puttin' him in check for disrespecting her, she was grinnin' and holdin' up the grocery line! That's one out of a million examples of keepin' it real ghetto!

All I'm saying is that there is a public decorum and mannerism that young people and adults should learn and practice. To carry yourself with dignity and self respect speaks volumes about you and your family. Impressions are usually lasting ones. Keepin' it real ghetto usually keeps you there.

Keepin' It Real Raunchy

It breaks my heart to hear and see some things that are being said and done by some youngins. I'm talkin' about freaky-deeky stuff! "Shake yo'..." ? Please! If some of ya'll mama's knew the stuff some of you youngins are into, listening to or lookin' at, they would faint! Some of ya'll keepin' it real raunchy!

I was flippin' channels one holiday and the most popular ghetto talk show was on. The theme of the program that day was, *"Who Got The Biggest Butt!"* Do you know sistas' were on stage showin' their butts to the audience and millions of viewers!

You got sistas on videos showin' thongs all up their crack, actin' like their brain is between their legs! To see and hear the degrading sexual songs sung by young brothas and sistas is keepin' it real raunchy - and raunchy is a mild term. I wonder how the preacher felt to see his daughter virtually naked on stage to get her Grammy? Youngins can break some parents' hearts up in here!

They say "sex sells." The message to gullible youngins is: *Sell yourself and you can become famous!* Those t.v. talk shows have become modern-day auction blocks and some record companies are modern-day slaveholders. Maybe that's why Prince wrote the word "slave" on his forehead during his protest. Keepin' it real raunchy is keepin' lots of youngins enslaved and degraded.

Keepin' It Real Sacreligious

A young person must have spiritual discernment if you are going to be able to identify what is real and what is fake. I believe a lot of youngins love Yahweh, but dishonor Yahweh at the same time. I trip when I hear youngins (who hype drugs, bangin', killin', use profanity and brag about screwin' somebody's brains out), get up on stage to accept an award and say, *"First of all, I want to thank God..."* That's keepin it real sacreligious!

I am not judging anybody, but I know Yahweh is not honored with all that "hipocracy!" **Whenever any person is misused, profaned, degraded or violated, it dishonors Yahweh.** What are they thanking Yahweh for? Yahweh didn't help them write those lyrics of degradation, profanity and vice! Yahweh didn't give them the inspiration to hype thug life, criminality and sexual perversion! (Maybe they're thanking Yahweh for not gettin' struck with lightening, rappin' that junk!)

Young people, don't be fooled by some platinum, cross-wearin' brothas or sistas whose lyrics and lifestyles are contrary to Yahweh's righteous will for our lives. **When it comes to true spirituality, "actions speak louder than words."** In fact, Yahshua Messiah says, *"Why call me Lord, and do not the things that I say?"* Another place in Scripture, Yahshua Messiah says, *"You draw near me with your lips, but your heart is far from Me."*

Don't be fooled youngins. I'm not judging them, but I am questioning their words versus their actions. Our Creator is not honored when we "talk the talk." Our Creator is honored when we "walk the talk."

Real or Fake (Myth)

I believe that a primary causative of insecure (fake) youngins is what some call *peer pressure*. **Peer pressure is simply accepting somebody else's myth of you.**

• You have given in to the pressure when you *dress* for the approval of others. Someone said, *"Most people buy clothes to impress people they don't even like!"* Whatever. But when what you wear becomes a way to get attention or acceptance, you are somebody else's myth, not your own reality.

• You have given in to the pressure when you *compromise* to get someone's approval. A brotha was right when he said, *"You don't have to compromise to be recognized."* When you do things you know are not right, just to be accepted, you are somebody else's myth, not your own reality.

• You have given in to the pressure when you *behave* a certain way to get someone's approval. Smoking or sellin' weed, drinking alcohol, hookin' school, fighting, and a host of other negative behaviors usually result from hanging with the wrong crowd. Any behavior that can cause you personal harm, endanger others or cause you to lose your freedom or your life, means you are somebody's myth, not your own reality.

• You have given in to the pressure when you are not working at your level of *academic excellence*. A lot of youngins have blown scholarships for college just to be accepted by youngins who have a scholarship to the penitentiary! Or when you are just interested in being an *athlete* instead of a *student-athlete*, which requires both academic and athletic excellence, you are giving in.

I can tell you from personal experience that not working at the level of your academic excellence will come back to haunt you one day. This is one huge area of future regret that is avoidable. But you have to be focused and avoid being side-tracked. When you don't work at your level of academic excellence, especially to be accepted by others, you are somebody's myth, not your own reality.

What Are Your "Pressure" Points?
The corporate-controlled media pressures you tenaciously in behalf of advertisers who pay them mad money. Some of you are to the point that if you don't own certain name brands or keep up with the latest trends, you feel inferior. When you feel pressure, it's usually to conform for someone else's profit or approval.

As it concerns certain relationships, there are some things you may feel pressured to do to get other's approval and some things you are not pressured with. Not knowing or dealing with your pressure points may be the reason many of you compromise, rationalize (or as someone said, "ration-lies") or don't put up strong opposition when the pressure is on.

What are your pressure points? *Is it to engage in premarital sexual activity? / Is it to get money by any means necessary - rob, steal, scheme or cheat? / Is it not to do your best in school so you won't be called a nerd? / Is it to wear the latest clothes or expensive jewelry? / Is it to keep the latest pair of athletic shoes? / Is it to go hard?/ Do you know your pressure points?*

Basing your self-image on the opinion of others because you think it offers you the approval of those you want to accept you or think well of you makes you an insecure person. The opinions of others are unstable and change according to how they feel about you at any given time. Basing your self-image on what you own to get the approval of others makes you an immature person.

It's sad to see young honeys chillin' with drug dealers - gold-diggin' - because they want the hair, shoes, nails, clothes - the prosperous look. But they got to give to get, and while they're gettin' what they want, they're not gettin' what they really need. Most of them just gettin' dogg-macked, jacked and whacked upside the head by these drug dealers!

You got to know your pressure points! Where are you feelin' pressure to do, to have or be somebody else's myth? Be honest.

How To Really Keep It Real?
1) **Know Who You Really Are**: Before you can have a positive and productive relationship with others, you must first have a relationship with yourself. Too many youngins are so busy trying to be what others want them to be that they become strangers to themselves.

I asked a group of young people to *tell me who you are* - one at a time. Do you know everyone of them told me their name! I did not ask them to tell me their name. I asked them to tell me who you are! That's the first question you must answer: Who are you? That question is not so easy to answer. It takes thought. *If you don't know who you are, you will definitely end up somebody else's myth!*

Saying that you grew up disadvantaged, your community was bad, and you didn't have such and such, makes you who you are, is not good enough. **Your upbringing and circumstances may have influenced *what* you are, but you are responsible for *who* you are and what you can become.**

2) **Know Your Real Purpose**: The African proverb says, *"If you don't know where you are going, any road will lead you there."* Our Creator gives each of us a purpose in life. **When you know your purpose, you will know when someone or something contradicts with your purpose.** You usually find your purpose in life by being other-people-minded. Your real purpose is not discovered in self-centeredness. *One of the best ways to discover your purpose in life is in service for others.*

When you find a need and fill it, something clicks, and you eventually discover what your real purpose is. Most people never fulfill their purpose in life. They just work and pay bills. Those who know their real purpose and follow through are most fulfilled in life. You can even tell the difference when you meet someone who knows their real purpose in life. They even vibe different. There not wanna be's. They're on a real mission.

3) **Know Real Fake and Separate.** If you are going to defeat the pressure, you got to know fake and separate. You can't be afraid

to walk alone. Too many youngins are locked down or have become "strange fruit" because of their associations. You can tell real fake because a person is trying to borrow somebody else's image instead of being themselves - like being from the suburbs but fakin' like they from the hood! You can peep them quick!

Or, you're from the hood, so you think you have to engage in negativity when you don't have to. You can be *in* the hood but not *of* the hood. *Weakness is not from without, but from within.* Just as salt has the ability to go down into fish and not become fish, you can live in the hood, but the hood don't have to live in you! So you fake 'cause you engage in negativity, but you don't have to.

Brothas fakin', sistas fakin' - "the whole world is a stage," as the famous line goes. If you don't have spiritual discernment, you will be faked out. You may end up dating or kickin' it with brothas or sistas that will be to your detriment.

You also need to have the courage to separate after you recognize fake. I procrastinated. That's when I made my biggest mistakes in life. Now I regret that I did not separate sooner. I lost four valuable years before I woke up and separated! I could have accomplished so much in four years. I'm still playin' catch up. It's not easy running four years behind your time allotted on earth. *The earlier you recognize real fake and separate, the less make up time you have to do - if you live to get another chance!*

4) **Know Real Haters**. They are the ones who always bring negativity, friction and trouble. Chill and listen to people, especially your associations. Listen to see if they talk negative all the time; *gossiping / complaining / whining / criticizing / puttin' people down / making excuses / foul mouth / lying / keepin' drama going on*. If so, they are the real haters.

Do they bring friction? / Do they keep having run-ins with youngins or starting trouble? / Are they on the revenge/pay back tip? / Are they always scheming on somebody? / Tryin' to play people? / Run games? If so, they are the real haters.

I believe that too many youngins think sistas and brothas like me are the real haters when we're not. *We're just tryin' to keep youngins on task / But you mistake our correction for criticism, when it's not / You misread our concern for condemnation, when it isn't / You think that because we accept no excuses that we are inflexible and unsympathetic, but that's not true.*

If you are going to move to the next level, you got to know real haters. You got to know the people who can help you get there from the people who will keep you from getting there. If you can't recognize real haters, then it will be difficult for you to recognize the people who really love you!

5) **Know Your Real Business.** What are your primary responsibilities? At home, at school, at work? Are you organized? Do you even own an organizer? ("Duh, what's an organizer?") It's something like a notebook that you can buy that has a daily calendar and other vital material to keep your business in order. An organizer should be your second Bible. It's just that important.

If you are to become more efficient and structured, you can't keep your business up in your head. You need an organizer that helps you develop an orderly, systematic method of handling your business. **The most important step in being organized is follow through.** You got to finish! What good is it written in your organizer if you don't follow through?

Let's go to the hoop for a minute. *You steal the ball and break away. You go the full length of the court and blow the lay up! Your buddies laugh hard while the crowd boos! What didn't you do? You didn't finish - as they say in the game. Not only do you have to finish, you got to finish strong!* The same goes for handling your real business. Follow through is quintessential. Without it, you are not handling your real business. If you're not organized, you can still recover by getting organized and following through.

What is your real business at hand? At home? In school? At work? Are you on task or are you slackin'? The habits you develop as a youth will follow you into adulthood like a pit bull chasing a mail man! If you are not learning and practicing organization and responsibility now, you better believe that it will bite you on the butt when you get to college! If you don't develop study habits now, it will hurt you later. And if you think that studying is the key when you get to college, then you are dead wrong. **The key to doing your best in college is time management**. Studying is very important, but it is the byproduct of time management.

Your professors will not be calling your home to tell your parents that you were not in class or you didn't turn in your assignment, like a concerned teacher did (or a recorded message) when your were in junior high or high school. You are given a syllabus in each of your classes. It tells your assignments and due dates. That's it. You're on your own. Now you got to handle your real business! But you got to bring your business with you. If you don't, you're gonna have to learn to take care of your business on the spot! That's handling your real business the hard way.

You need more than a good memory to maintain academic excellence. *You need to get organized now / You need to learn how to study, how to take notes and how to read with comprehension now / You need to learn time management now*. There are methods for learning these things. There are books in the library that can teach you these necessary skills. You can also talk to a friend who is in college now. They should be able to give you good insight.

Finally, you have business at home and at work. The foundation for learning responsibility begins in your home. *It's doing your chores / It's seeing what needs to be done around the house and doing it without being told / It's not being afraid to do more work than your brother or sister / It's not being afraid to do hard work - without complaining.*

One of the most important attributes you must bring to adulthood is a good work ethic. Let me share with you five traits of a person with good work ethic. 1) When there is a job to do, you don't mind doing the hardest task. 2) If you don't' know how to do something, you don't shy away from it, you ask someone to show you how to do it. 3) You don't quit. You complete the job you started. 4) You do such quality work that you can be given a task and your supervisor knows that it will be done right and well. 5) You don't just learn your job. Get as much knowledge about the jobs others are doing around you so you understand the "big picture" and see how your job fits into the whole scheme of things. Such knowledge gives you a better perspective of your job.

Get organized / Follow through / Be responsible / Manage your time / Acquire a good work ethic / Understand the big picture. Whether it's home, school or work. Know your real business.

6) **Know How To Stay Real Focused.** Following someone else's myth distracts you. The "crowd" of voices and choices constantly beckon young people in their direction. It's easy to get sidetracked. That's why *knowing who you really are, knowing your real purpose, knowing real fake and separating, knowing real haters and knowing your real business* is of utmost importance. It helps to keep you real focused.

I was reading why animal trainers carry certain objects into a lion's cage. When they are trying to get a lion to sit on the stool or to perform other tricks for the audience, they have a whip in one hand; they also have a pistol strapped to their waist. But it is said that the most important piece of equipment animal trainers carry into the cage is the chair. They hold it by the back and they thrust the legs toward the face of the wild animal. It's because the animal tries to focus on all four legs at once. In their attempt to focus on all four legs, a kind of paralysis overwhelms the animal and it becomes tame, weak and disabled, simply because its attention is divided!

When you lose your focus, you become weak, and when you are weak, your power of resistance is diminished. When your power of resistance is diminished, you may fall for anything! The "crowd" is in a constant and unending struggle to break your focus. Soon, you no longer think for yourself because the crowd decides for you. If the crowd approves, you're down, but if the crowd disapproves, (even if it's good for you) it's out.

Don't be misled. The majority has never ruled! It has always, and continues to be a small minority who are the movers and shakers. The real deal is that the majority is ruled! If you follow the crowd of voices and choices, you will lose your real focus. The crowd focuses on too many things at one time. That's one of the reasons the crowd is so dissatisfied in life. When you follow steps 1-5, it will not be difficult to step out of the crowd and keep your real focus. You are also in the best position for step 7.

7) Know How To Be Real Spiritual

There has never been a time in history that humans have not worshiped someone or something. Whether you realize it or not, you will give your devotion to someone or something. That's because we were created to worship. We were created to worship our Creator. But we have been given the power of choice. Our Creator didn't make us robots. We can choose to worship someone or something other than our Creator.

A lot of youngins worship money. There's nothing they won't do to get money. That's worship. Some youngins worship clothes and jewelry. That's their #1 devotion. That's worship. Some honey's worship nails and hair. They will go without essentials but will not go without having their nails and hair done. Whatever. Whoever or whatever gets our *highest* devotion is our object of worship.

As far as "religion" is concerned, a lot of youngins are turned off to organized religion. The number one turn-off for youngins is "hypocrisy." A whole lot of religious people are fakin'. Like the song Take 6 sings, *"One night of praying and six nights of fun, the odds of going to heaven are 6 to 1!"* When it comes to religion, most youngins don't want to be fake, so they keep their distance from it.

But there is just as much "hipocracy" going on in Hip-Hop culture as it is in organized religion, maybe even more. Drugs, violence, misogyny, disrespect, sexual immorality, killing, glorification of materialism, and so much more. Is that any better than the hypocrisy that goes on in all religions?

The word hypocrisy in the dictionary comes from the word *hypokrites*, which means, *"playing an act on stage."* In my opinion, that's what a lot of people in religion and youngins in Hip-Hop culture are doing - acting! It's all an act being perpetrated as genuine. If you are fake in religion or Hip-Hop culture, you're still a "hipocrite."

Spirituality is different from religion. *But any so-called spirituality that does not have at its center obeying Yahweh's natural and spiritual principles, is not true spirituality.* We are more than physical and mental beings - we also have the capacity to be spiritual. It is the spiritual part of us that connects with our Creator. The spiritual part is to direct our mental and physical life.

Real spirituality is not endowed, it is acquired. Becoming a real spiritual person is a personal desire and decision. You can't get it from your parents, no matter how righteous they are. Spirituality is not something you inherit from them. Spirituality is something you acquire for yourself out of a personal decision to live a life that honors Yahweh and respect for Yahweh's creation.

So often, young people get disillusioned as they get older. Say for instance you came up in the "church." As you got older, you noticed more hypocrisy and started getting turned off. As you got old enough to think for yourself and not accept everything you heard in church, you started questioning some of the teachings.

Later, you learned the truth that Yahshua Messiah (so-called Jesus) was not a European white man, but a man of African ancestry and color. You began to wonder, what else is not true? The caucasian image that you were shown as a child turned out to be a hoax and you started to question religion a whole lot more after that. After while, some youngins leave the church.

I know youngins are on a search for more truth. And because aspects of truth are addressed in Hip-Hop culture, primarily by rappers, (in addition to the fashions, etc.) youngins who are searching for more truth gravitate to them. But without practicing Yahweh's natural and spiritual principles, truth alone is not enough. The blessing is that you have the opportunity to acquire real spirituality for yourself. Real spirituality is the anchor that keeps you stable in an unstable world. Real spirituality dictates your choices and associations. If you disregard real spirituality, you will not be complete as a person.

Money and materials have their place, but they can't complete you. Only our Creator can make you complete, but you have to follow His natural and spiritual principles. Take for example, a car. A car has a designer. That designer provides an owners manuel to give instructions on the optimum operation of the car. The designer knows what is best for the car - the type of gas, oil, and other essentials the car needs to operate efficiently. If you disregard the owners manual the car will not function properly and you will lessen the longevity of the car.

The same principle applies to real spirituality. Our Creator knows what's best for all creation. Crops need sunlight and water. Animals need a certain environment and food. Humans need our Creator's natural and spiritual principles to acquire a complete, healthy, spiritual life. Let me show you how to begin to keep it real spiritual. I'm not gonna preach. It's only two steps.

The first step to begin real spirituality is to believe that there is a Creator. There are people who believe in evolution. They believe that there was a "big bang" and things evolved to what they now are. Somebody cynically said, "It's like a great wind blew through a scrap yard and out came a Rolls Royce!" Nothing happens by chance. There is always a decision behind it. If there is a law, there must first be a Lawgiver. If there is a creation, there must first be a Creator.

Real spirituality begins by believing there is a Creator. You can only do that by exercising faith. Faith is something you believe even when you can't see it with your eyes or fully understand it with your mind. If you can have faith to believe there was a El Hajj Malik El Shabazz (formerly Malcolm X), or a Sojourner Truth, even though you never saw them, then you can use the same faith to believe there is a Creator. (As you have noticed, I use the African Hebrew name, Yahweh). Believing that Yahweh exists is half of becoming real spiritual.

The second step in real spirituality is to believe that Yahweh is the REWARDER of those who diligently seek Him. Here is where your faith becomes action. You have to choose to seek after Yahweh. In any relationship, you have to communicate and spend quality time getting to know the person. When you have a good relationship, you also want to tell people about it.

You communicate with Yahweh through prayer, talking as if you would to a best friend. Just as you tell your friend of your joys, challenges, and hurts. You ask for wisdom and guidance. You thank them often for their love and acceptance, even when you make mistakes. You also admit when you wrong them and ask for forgiveness so your relationship can be restored back to normal. Do the same thing with Yahweh.

Next, you "diligently" seek Yahweh by having a sincere desire to know the truth, the whole truth and nothing but the truth. There are truths in the principles of nature. There are truths in spiritual principles. Gravity is an example of a natural principle (truth). The Ten Commandments (Exodus 20:1-17) are an example of spiritual principles (truths). You have to seek these truths out and study them for yourself (or in a group). It is by the studying of natural and spiritual principles that you find out Yahweh's plan for humanity.

As you apply these principles to your life, you will see how Yahweh will work in your life, help you work out your challenges, and position you to be rewarded with all the blessings, opportunities, privileges and benefits our Creator has for your life. That's real spirituality in a nutshell.

Love is the foundation of real spirituality. The more you love, the less you want to dishonor our Creator. And when you learn to truly love yourself, you won't need the approval of someone else to validate you. **"If you are not your own reality, whose myth are you?"**

Playa's Paradise?

"Is a playa' still a playa' after the judge says, "Life without parole?"

The justice system in America has always been cruel to people of color. As we use to say back in the day, justice in America is really "just-us" when it comes to arresting and locking people up. Go into the average criminal court room during the week and you will see "just-us." I'm not saying that African American and African Caribbean people don't commit crimes. Some do, but we are disproportionally arrested and incarcerated, but it's not "just-us" committing crimes! You don't need glasses to see that!

So-called "white collar crime" consists largely of white males (and a few white females) who work for multinational corporations. But white collar criminals are not tried in criminal court, even though they have committed atrocious crimes. They are prosecuted in civil court. Consequently, 89% of white collar criminals never see any prison time. And the average prison time served by a white collar criminal is 15 months! These criminals can embezzle millions, get fined a few hundred thousand dollars by the court, get probation and live off the rest of the stolen millions! Can African American men or women catch a break like that? Never!

The local, state and federal courts have become ultra-conservative and blatantly mean-spirited as it relates to African American youth. It's a lock-them-up-and-throw-away-the-key mentality! But here's what I can't understand. Even though youngins know the courts are vicious on them, many of these youngins act like they want to go to prison! Duh? Some youngins act like it's a badge of honor to get locked down! *They act like they're going to a "playa's paradise!"*

A lot of these prisons they are being sent to got mad history. Attica, Pelican Bay, San Quentin, Greaterford and Rahway, to name a few. These prisons ain't no joke either! That includes women's prisons too! These prisons are no playa's paradise! They are not for rehabilitating you and putting you back into society as law abiding and productive citizens. They are called "penal" institutions. They are designed to *penalize* you to the fullest extent.

But while youngins are being penalized, certain people are profiting big time off of them! There are people who want so-called playas' locked down. They are contributing to political campaigns and electing politicians that boast being "tough on crime." They are writing laws that are helping greedy people to live large! *Law and order has always taken a back seat to money!*

I know this injustice system is messed up and there are endless reforms that we must continue to fight for. Having said that, I will never condone any crime committed by so-called playas'. I'm playa' hatin' the youngins and old-heads who are stealing, killing, assaulting, shooting, selling drugs, breaking and entering, and all the other crimes they are committing! Committing crime is wrong. My mother said, "If it's wrong the first time, then it's wrong every time." They need their roll slowed!

In this chapter, I want you to see the picture behind the picture. Youngins need to understand that politics and economics are bed-fellows in the prison industrial complex. Let me show you how playas' are being played.

For-Profit Prisons

There are corporations who are making mad money off of lock-ing down Youngins! You would be surprised to know some of the corporations who are investing in prisons! The more inmates, the more private prisons; the more private prisons, the more money they make. **Most youth don't know that the prison industrial complex is one of the fastest grossing commodities on the stock market!** Private prisons are big business!

Corrections Corporation of America (CCA) is the nation's largest provider of detention and corrections services to govern-mental agencies. Founded in 1983, CCA pioneered a new indus-try - private sector corrections. CCA's full range of services include design, construction, ownership, renovation and management of new or existing jails and prisons, as well as long distance inmate transportation services.

Today, CCA is the industry leader in private sector corrections with over 52% of the domestic market. CCA has well-known investors such as the Sodexho-Marriott Services. Carefully selecting the most lucrative prison contracts, slashing labor costs and various other strategies caused the value of CCA's shares to soar from $50 million in 1986 to more than $3.5 billion in 1997! The company controls about half of the private prison industry in the U.S. and worldwide.

Sodexho sometimes tries to distance itself from CCA. "We own no prisons. We operate no prisons," said a spokesperson for Sodexho's U.S. subsidiary, Sodexho Marriott Services. However, Sodexho Alliance owns 48% of Sodexho Marriott Services and owns shares in CCA. Moreover, CCA and Sodexho Alliance openly acknowledge that they have been involved in an "international strategic alliance" since 1994 to pursue prison profiteering opportunities outside the U.S.

CCA and Sodexho Alliance each have 50% ownership of Corrections Corporation of Australia and United Kingdom Detention Services and plan to participate in future international joint ventures! CCA has also operated a private prison in Puerto Rico since 1995. CCA-Australia has also operated, since 1996, the first private women's prison in the world outside of the U.S.

Australia was an obvious target for CCA and Sodexho where the prison population there increased by 300% for women and 150% for men from 1976 to 1998. And you better believe that these are people of color who are getting locked down in Australia!

I'm just trying to get you youngins to see that there is an international move on people of color by the prison industrial complex. It's not about law and order (odor - as I call it). It's all about the Benjamins! There are politicians and judges who are down with these for profit prison corporations!

Conflicts of interest abound in private prisons. For example, prison authorities hold considerable influence over the outcome of parole hearings, and private operators might find it profitable to extend a prisoner's sentence. Private operators might also find it profitable to down-play problems, so as to avoid penalty provisions stipulated in their contracts.

Prison privatization also allows governments to avoid responsibility for the running of the criminal justice system, while allowing private companies to exert influence over law and order policies, through lobbying, donating to political parties or whipping up law and order hysteria through the media.

Any attempt by governments at genuine reform of the "law and order" system might also be thwarted or limited by contractual obligations to private prison operators. Public oversight is hampered by the greater-than-usual secrecy in private prisons, justified by "commercial confidentiality," and by frequent use of threats of defamation action against critics and the media.

I want you youngins to understand that the prison industrial complex considers *playas'* more than just criminals. They see playas' as a dollar $ign - an investment that will bring big returns in their corporate and personal bank accounts!

A survey commissioned by the National Institute of Justice identified more than 70 companies that "employ" inmates in 16 states in manufacturing, service and light assembly operations. Prisoners sew leisure wear, manufacture water-bed mattresses and assemble electronic components. PRIDE, a state-sponsored private corporation that runs Florida's 46 prison industries - from furniture making to optical glass grinding - made a $4 million profit in way back in 1987. Imagine what they are making off the labor of prisoners now!

By the end of 1996, the Private Sector Prison Industry Enhancement program had nearly 100 private firms "employing" just over 2,000 prison inmates to manufacture goods ranging from circuit boards to bird feeders to graduation gowns. Airline reservations, telemarketing, data processing and map digitizing services are also done by prisoners. Corporations are profiting big time off of "playa' labor" in prisons! Need a job playa'?

Is Prison A Playa's Paradise?

What trips me out is the thug mentality thinks getting locked down enhances their status among other so-called thugs. Whatever Young! But something is wrong with that picture! The truth is that young people don't understand how vicious this injustice system actually is toward youth. There are draconian laws in place, and the Republican-controlled Congress are crafting more punitive laws!

And appointed to the presidency by the majority Supreme Court is the man who presided over the most death penalty executions in American history, as governor of Texas! Youngins, you don't want to get locked down now! I need to educate you. And you need to know.

Juvenile Justice System

Before I talk about the Juvenile Justice Bill that advocates prosecuting juveniles in adult courts, you need to know some history about the juvenile justice system.

The first court designed specifically to deal with children was established in Chicago one hundred years ago and led to the development of a separate juvenile justice system nationwide. Juvenile courts are responsible for dealing with children who are accused of committing two types of offenses: *Status offenses* and *Delinquency offenses.* Status offenses are violations of laws with which only children can be charged (e.g., running away from home). Delinquency offenses are acts committed by a child which, if committed by an adult, could result in criminal prosecution.

The premise on which the separate juvenile system rested was that children are developmentally different from adults and thus are more amenable to treatment and rehabilitation. The juvenile justice process centered on the individual child and took into account the child's problems and needs, focusing less on punishment than on helping the child to change and so minimize the likelihood of future criminal behavior.

Congress in 1996, has undermined the traditional practice of treating young offenders as different from adult criminals – less culpable because of their age and more amenable to rehabilitation. *In recent years, the focus has turned to punishment and in particular to the transfer of increasing numbers of youthful offenders from juvenile to criminal courts.*

In recent years, fear of juvenile crime and criminals has undermined the basic concepts on which the juvenile court was founded. State legislatures and the federal government have turned increasingly to the more punitive adult model, requiring that even pre-teen children in some instances be treated as if they were equal in culpability and understanding to adults who commit similar crimes.

These so-called solutions have done more harm than good. This policy to prosecute juveniles in adult court is another failed 'get tough" policy which is unjust and harmful to children and does nothing to increase public safety.

It has been argued that the large sudden increase in gun killing was tied to the development of crack markets in the inner city where fierce turf wars are waged and juveniles are actively recruited by the organizers of these markets. As more guns were put on the streets, more juveniles began to carry them for self-defense and the number of deaths spiraled.

Legislative actions in recent years have emphasized measures requiring harsher punishment of juveniles. Following the Columbine school shootings in April 1999, the Senate added some gun control measures to the juvenile justice bill then under consideration in Congress. This juvenile justice bill would:

- Allow youth as young as 13 to be tried as adults in the federal court system.
- Expand the range of federal crimes for which a juvenile can be prosecuted as an adult.
- Provide for additional mandatory sentences for juveniles in federal court.
- Reduce the restrictions on the housing of juveniles in adult

prisons and jails.

Both state and federal legislative responses to juvenile crime have focused on sending more and younger children to adult criminal courts. Since 1992, almost every state has made it easier to try juveniles as adults. Congress provided additional encouragement to this trend in 1998 by making some federal money contingent on states having policies allowing for the prosecution of those over the age of 14 as adults.

State juvenile codes have long permitted the most serious, chronic or older youthful offenders to be transferred to the adult criminal court by a process of judicial "waiver" following a hearing in front of a judge in juvenile court. However, in recent years there have been significant changes in the processes by which juvenile offenders end up in adult court. A disproportionate number of children of color are prosecuted as adults. Latest statistics from the Department of Justice show that:

• 67% of juvenile defendants in adult court are African American
• 77% of juveniles sent to adult prison are persons of color (60% African American, 15% Hispanic, 1% Native American, 1% Asian)
• 75% of juvenile defendants charged with drug offenses in adult court are African American
• 95% of juveniles sentenced to adult prison for drug offenses are persons of color.

Juveniles who receive custodial sentences in the criminal court usually serve their sentences in adult prisons and jails. Juveniles in adult facilities, particularly in jails, frequently do not receive the education or other services appropriate to their age and needs.

Juveniles in adult correctional facilities suffer higher rates of physical and sexual abuse and suicide. Compared to those held in juvenile detention centers, youth held in adult jails are:

• 7.7 times more likely to commit suicide
• Twice as likely to be beaten by staff
• 50% more likely to be attacked with a weapon
• 5 times more likely to be sexually assaulted

It is estimated based on previously published surveys that some

80,000 unwanted sexual acts take place behind bars in the United States every day, with a total of 364,000 prisoners raped every year! 242,000 of them are sexually penetrated!

Prisoner rape is torture -- the infliction of severe emotional and/or physical pain as punishment and/or coercion. Long after the body has healed, the emotions remain traumatized, shamed and stigmatized. The psychological effects of prisoner rape can last a lifetime and often lead to substance abuse, domestic violence and much worse. Most prisoners on death row were sexually abused earlier in life.

Suicide is the leading cause of death behind bars. Sexual assault is the leading cause of suicide in confinement. California leads the nation in prisoner suicides. Besides psychosis and suicide, other side effects of prisoner rape are murder, AIDS, and recidivism. Prisoner rape can be greatly reduced at no extra cost to taxpayers by separating the obviously vulnerable prisoners from the obviously violent ones and by more vigilant staff.

Adult courts are inappropriate and unjust settings for the disposition of juvenile cases. Furthermore, the imposition of adult punishments, far from deterring crime, actually increases the likelihood that a young person will commit further criminal offenses. The transfer of increasing numbers of children from juvenile to criminal courts is continuing in the face of mounting evidence of the harm it does both to the children and to public safety.

In addition to receiving an adult sentence and possibly serving time in an adult prison, juveniles convicted in criminal court may suffer other long-term legal consequences. Depending on the laws of their state, a juvenile tried as an adult may:

• Be subject to criminal court jurisdiction for any subsequent offense committed as a juvenile
• Have their conviction a matter of public record
• Have to report their conviction on employment applications
• Lose the right to serve in the military
• Lose the right to vote - sometimes for life!

An estimated 3.9 million Americans, or one in fifty adults,

have currently or permanently lost their voting rights as a result of a felony conviction. Given current rates of incarceration, three in ten of the next generation of African American men can expect to be disenfranchised at some point in their lifetime. In states that disenfranchise ex-offenders, as many as 40% of African American men may permanently lose their right to vote.

Let's take a look at some of the punitive laws on the books and see if it's worth being a thug or a playa'!

Three Strikes and You're Out!

Following the passage of the nation's first *"3 Strikes And You're Out"* law in Washington state in 1993, legislators across the country have developed proposals to adopt similar policies. At the federal level, a similar proposal adopted in the 1993 Senate crime bill requires *life without parole* not only for third-time violent offenders, but also for third-time drug offenders or for offenses involving a threat to property. Serious violent offenses -- murder, rape, armed robbery -- are punishable by sentences up to life in prison or the death penalty in almost all states.

Racial Disparity in Sentencing

Research has consistently shown that sentencing disparity is based on race. Studies have demonstrated that this discretion results in different outcomes based on race, quality of defense attorney, and other factors not related to public safety.

Approximately 2/3 of crack users are white or Hispanic, yet the vast majority of persons convicted of possession in federal courts are African American. In one year, of the defendants convicted of crack possession:

• 84.5% were African American, 10.3% were white, and 5.2% were Hispanic.

Of those who were convicted of selling crack:

• 88.3% were African American, 7.1% were Hispanic and 4.1% were white.

The result of the combined difference in sentencing laws and racial disparity is that African American men and women are serving longer prison sentences than white men and women.

Crack/Cocaine Sentencing Laws

In 1986 and 1988 Congress adopted *mandatory sentencing laws* on crack in the wake of widespread media attention. These laws were based on the idea that crack is 50 times more addictive than powder cocaine. The psychotropic (mood altering) and physiological effects of all types of cocaine are the same, but the intensity and duration of the high differ according to the way it is taken. Crack is always smoked and gives a fast, intense high. Powder cocaine is usually snorted, which gives a slower and less intense high.

Although the two types of cocaine cause similar physical reactions, the sentences that users and sellers of the drugs face are vastly different. For powder cocaine, a conviction of possession with intent to distribute carries a five year sentence for quantities of 500 grams or more. But for crack, a conviction of possession with intent to distribute carries a five year sentence for only 5 grams (the weight of two pennies).

This is a 100-to-1 quantity ratio. **Crack is also the only drug that carries a mandatory prison sentence for first offense possession.** A person convicted in federal court of possession of 5 grams of crack automatically receives a 5 year prison term. A person convicted of possessing 5 grams of powder cocaine will probably receive a probation sentence.

Crack was portrayed as a violence inducing, highly addictive plague of inner cities, and this media spotlight led to the quick passage of two federal sentencing laws concerning crack cocaine in 1986 and 1988. The laws created a 100:1 quantity ratio between the amount of crack and powder cocaine needed to trigger certain mandatory minimum sentences for trafficking, as well as creating a mandatory minimum penalty for simple possession of crack cocaine. *The result of these laws is that crack users and dealers receive much harsher penalties than users and dealers of powder cocaine.*

The U.S. Sentencing Commission has estimated that 5 grams of crack has a street value of approximately $500. Locking up such an offender in the federal prison system for five years at an average annual minimal cost of $25,000 results in a taxpayer expense of $125,000.

Studies conducted by the Rand Corporation have documented that investing in drug treatment would reduce serious crime fifteen times more than expanding the use of federal mandatory sentences and would be three times as cost-effective in reducing drug use, sales and drug-related crime.

• Incarcerating a drug addict - $25,000 a year
• A year of traditional outpatient drug treatment - $1,800
• Intensive outpatient care - $2,500
• Methadone treatment for heroin users - $3,900
• Residential drug treatment - $4,000 - $6,800 a year

The crack/cocaine sentencing laws are unjustified and unreasonable. This is a good place for young people to start youth advocacy groups to have these disparity laws changed. With so many youth (some of your friends) being convicted of crack distribution and going to prison (not paradise), you can and must make a difference. As someone said, "Silence is not always golden, sometimes it's merely yellow!"

Since 1970, the number of Americans behind bars has increased by more than 500% and is expected to reach 2,000,000 in 2001. The bulk of the newly incarcerated are young people of color (age 15-30) from urban neighborhoods who have been convicted of non-violent drug offenses.

The impact of prison expansion on youth, families and communities is devastating. Each day there are young people who lose opportunities, families and even lives - yet the "war" on people of color grinds on with no clear objective and no end in sight. Yet, until there is broad-based public understanding of the issues and a grassroots movement capable of holding elected officials accountable, the politicians will continue to pander to perceived public fears and to the real economic interests of corporations and others that profit from prison expansion.

Drug Conspiracy Law

Q. If you know about illegal drug activities, but are not directly involved, can you be prosecuted?

A. If there is an implied or expressed agreement between two or more people to violate the drug laws, they can be prosecuted for conspiracy to violate drug laws. Driving someone to make a drug transaction, or letting them use your car to purchase drugs can make you part of a drug conspiracy. Even if you did not possess, sell or profit from the drugs. **Conspiracy convictions carry the same penalties as if the offense was actually committed.**

The following are sad but true stories about young people who were charged with drug conspiracy. This tragic story was in the Washington Post.

Lamont and Lawrence Garrison were having their grandmother's car worked on at an auto body shop in Maryland owned by T.A. T.A. used the shop as a front for his drug dealing operation and didn't work on the car for months. The brothers repeatedly called to find out when the car would be ready but never got an answer. T.A. and 20 co-defendants were arrested for conspiracy to distribute powder and crack cocaine. T.A. implicated the twins to reduce his lengthy sentence and was given 36 months. Lamont and Lawrence, believing their innocence, took their case to trial and lost. Lamont was given 15 years with an extra four years because he testified that he and his brother were innocent in court. Lawrence was given 15 years!

- Lamont's sentence: 19 years x $25,000 per year = $475,000
- Lawrence's sentence: 15 years x $25,000 per year = $375,000
- Charge: Conspiracy to distribute crack cocaine
- No prior felonies; college graduates, aspiring lawyers

Kemba Smith was a sophomore in college when she met Peter Hall, a smooth talker who swept her off her feet. She became Peter's girlfriend, initially unaware that he was a drug dealer. Peter became very possessive and violent with Kemba, beating her badly and threatening her and her parent's lives if she told what was happening. Eventually Kemba found out she was fac-

ing federal charges for alleged involvement in Peter's drug ring. She turned herself in, knowing she was innocent of selling drugs. Shortly thereafter, Peter was found murdered. Although prosecutors said that Kemba never used, held, or sold drugs, she was held accountable for the entire amount of cocaine – 225 kilograms – allegedly distributed by Peter and his associates during the entire conspiracy. Kemba's sentence was higher than her codefendants, who actually sold the drugs. Kemba was sentenced to 24 years and 6 months!

- Kemba's sentence: 24 years, six months x $25,000 a year = $600,000
- Charge: Conspiracy to distribute crack cocaine, lying to federal authorities, and money laundering
- No prior felonies; college student, one child

I had the privilege of meeting Kemba's parents at the *Annual Conference On The African American Family* in Huntsville, Alabama. They are on a mission, traveling the country, talking to young people about Kemba's Nightmare, the unfair maximum/minimum laws, and encouraging young people to the make good choices and choose good associates.

Kemba Smith was released from federal prison December 22, 2000. Her petition for clemency was signed by President Bill Clinton. Kemba had served 6 years of a 24 1/2-year sentence, longer than the average state sentence for murder! Kemba and her family expressed thanks to all the people who stepped forward to protest her unjust sentencing and to work in the struggle for Justice. You can read the whole intriguing ordeal of Kemba Smith in two back issues of Emerge Magazine (May 1996 and May 1998.)

Obviously with these laws, African American females are being locked down in increasing numbers. Most women are jailed for non-violent offenses such as larceny, petty theft, forgery, welfare fraud, prostitution and drug convictions. *Nationally, three out of one hundred African American women are in prison, on probation or parole.*

Unlike men, more than eighty percent of imprisoned women are single parents. More than one million children have a mother who is in prison. More than 200,000 children were sent to foster homes or agencies after their mother was incarcerated. *Children denied the parental bonding, nurturing, and affection that comes from sustained contact with their mother are more likely to become self-destructive to themselves and menaces to society, unless their extended family takes them in, supports and rears them.*

Racial Profiling

Today skin color makes you a suspect in America. It makes you more likely to be stopped, more likely to be searched, and more likely to be arrested and imprisoned.

Racial profiling is a law enforcement strategy that police officers use to stop and question African-Americans simply because of their race. Racial profiling is inherently biased in its basic assumption that African Americans are more likely to commit crimes than other people of color or whites. This assumption has precipitated numerous, documented incidents of police brutality against people of color.

Racial profiling took off during the highly publicized explosion of crack cocaine in inner-city neighborhoods in the 1980s, which bolstered the perception of drugs as a black problem -- even though statistics show most cocaine users are white.

Drug enforcement agencies began using racial profiling to "sweep" neighborhoods and arrest disproportionate numbers of African-Americans for drug-related offenses. Racial profiling has given police a lame excuse to target people who they think fit a "drug courier" or "gang member" profile. Please!

Recent high-profile cases and studies of racial profiling in New Jersey and Maryland prompted African American Congressman John Conyers to introduce the Traffic Stops Statistics Study Act of 1999, directing Attorney General Janet Reno to conduct a nationwide study of the race of drivers who are stopped by law enforcement. Congress is expected to vote on the bill in the 2001 Congress.

• African-Americans are almost five times more likely to be

stopped on the New Jersey Turnpike than people of other races. In Maryland, 71.3 percent of those searched by state police on Interstate 95 are African-Americans. (The whole 95 Interstate - from New England to Florida is a racial profile trap!)

When racial profiling is used as a tactic in law enforcement, law-abiding African-Americans justly fear for their safety and freedom. Racial profiling fuels mistrust and anger in African American communities toward law enforcement because the policy proliferates police brutality and institutional racism in police forces nationwide.

DWB

Driving While Black (DWB) is the popular term that's used when referring to the disproportionate traffic stops by law enforcement officers. Civil rights organizations are supporting legislation that will stop this human rights violation. If you are an African American male, nine times out of ten, you're gonna get stopped! You need to know your rights! You also need to know how to conduct yourself during a traffic or highway stop by a law enforcement officer. That goes for you sistas' too.

The NAACP, the Congressional Black Caucus, and other African American organizations have taken up the fight against racial profiling. The American Civil Liberties Union is actively challenging the illegalities of racial profiling. There is a lot of pertinent information on their web site. I got the following information from their site. They've come up with a "Bustcard" that gives you guidelines when you encounter law enforcement officers. I suggest that you keep a copy in your car. Share this information with your friends. Read and heed! It may save your life!

What To Do If You Are Stopped By Law Enforcement
• Be polite and respectful. Never bad-mouth a police officer
• Stay calm and in control of your words, body language and emotions
• Don't get into an argument with the police
• Remember, anything you say or do can be used against you

- Keep your hands where the police can see them
- Don't run. Don't touch any police officer
- Don't resist even if you believe you are innocent
- Don't complain on the scene or tell the police they're wrong or that you're going to file a complaint
- Do not make any statements regarding the incident. Ask for a lawyer immediately upon your arrest
- Remember officers' badge & patrol car numbers
- Write down everything you remember as soon as possible
- Try to find witnesses and get their names & phone numbers
- If you are injured, take photographs of the injuries as soon as possible, but make sure you seek medical attention first
- If you feel your rights have been violated, file a written complaint with police department's internal affairs division or civilian complaint board

If You Have A Police Encounter, You Can Protect Yourself
1. What you say to the police is always important. What you say can be used against you, and it can give the police an excuse to arrest you, especially if you bad-mouth a police officer.
2. You don't have to answer a police officer's questions, but you must show your driver's license and registration when stopped in a car. In other situations, you can't legally be arrested for refusing to identify yourself to a police officer.
3. You don't have to consent to any search of yourself, your car or your house. If you do consent to a search, it can affect your rights later in court. If the police say they have a search warrant, **ask to see it**.
4. Do not interfere with, or obstruct the police -- you can be arrested for it.

If You Are Stopped For Questioning
1. It's not a crime to refuse to answer questions, but refusing to answer can make the police suspicious about you. You can't be arrested merely for refusing to identify yourself on the street.
2. Police may "pat-down" your clothing if they suspect a con-

cealed weapon. Don't physically resist, but make it clear that you don't consent to any further search.

3. Ask if you are under arrest. If you are, you have a right to know why.

4. Don't bad-mouth the police officer or run away, even if you believe what is happening is unreasonable. That could lead to your arrest.

If You Are Stopped In Your Car

1. Upon request, show them your drivers license, registration, and proof of insurance. In certain cases, your car can be searched without a warrant as long as the police have probable cause. To protect yourself later, you should make it clear that you do not consent to a search. It is not lawful for police to arrest you simply for refusing to consent to a search.

2. If you're given a ticket, you should sign it; otherwise you can be arrested. You can always fight the case in court later.

3. If you're suspected of drunk driving (DUI) and refuse to take a blood, urine or breath test, your driver's license may be suspended.

If You Are Arrested Or Taken To A Police Station

1. You have the right to remain silent and to talk to a lawyer before you talk to the police. Tell the police nothing except your name and address. Don't give any explanations, excuses or stories. You can make your defense later, in court, based on what you and your lawyer decide is best.

2. Ask to see a lawyer immediately. If you can't pay for a lawyer, you have a right to a free one, and should ask the police how the lawyer can be contacted. Don't say anything without a lawyer.

3. Within a reasonable time after your arrest, or booking, you have the right to make a local phone call - to a lawyer, bail bondsman, a relative or any other person. The police may not listen to the call to the lawyer.

4. Sometimes you can be released without bail, or have bail lowered. Have your lawyer ask the judge about this possibility. You

must be taken before the judge on the next court day after arrest.
5. Do not make any decisions in your case until you have talked
with a lawyer.

In Your Home
1. If the police knock and ask to enter your home, you don't have
to admit them unless they have a warrant signed by a judge.
2. However, in some emergency situations (like when a person is
screaming for help inside, or when the police are chasing someone) officers are allowed to enter and search your home without
a warrant.
3. If you are arrested, the police can search you and the area close
by. If you are in a building, "close by" usually means just the
room you are in.

We all recognize the need for effective law enforcement, but we
should also understand our own rights and responsibilities --
especially in our encounters with the police. Everyone, including
minors, has the right to courteous and respectful police treatment.

If your rights are violated, don't try to deal with the situation at
the scene. You can discuss the matter with an attorney afterwards,
or file a complaint with the Internal Affairs or Civilian Complaint
Board.

Note: You can go online on the American Civil Liberties Union
(ACLU) web site and electronically fill out the **Driver Profiling
Complaint Form.**

Death Penalty
Right now, more than 3,500 inmates sit on Death Row in America. Almost all are poor, and a wildly disproportionate number are
people of color. In addition, most had legal representation that
ranged from inadequate to grossly incompetent.

One hundred-fifty people have been executed in Texas since
George W. Bush became Governor of Texas in 1995. The Lone
Star state holds the U.S. record with 40 executions in one year.
Now that he has been appointed president and John Ashcroft is
his Attorney General, look for courts to become more punitive by

limiting death row inmate appeals and speeding up executions.

The process of being placed on death row varies from state-to-state. Usually, a death row inmate is locked down 23 of 24 hours of the day. Death row is a breeding ground of insanity for weakening inmates.

I want you to read Mumia Abu-Jamal's book, *"Live From Death Row."* In 1982, Mumia was convicted and sentenced to death for the murder of a Philadelphia police office. Even though there are mounds of evidence that points to his innocence, he has been denied a retrial and is in the final stage of his appeal to the U.S. Supreme Court. If denied, Mumia will be executed.

John Edgar Wideman writes the Introduction to Mumia's book. Wideman says, *"Live From Death Row is an unflinching account of the brutalities, humiliations and atrocities of prison life - the full body-cavity searches before each visit, the smell of charred flesh from a fellow inmate who can take no more of "the hole" and burns himself to death, the outrage of a young daughter who, because of enforced separation by glass during visits has not touched her father in twelve years."*

Can you imagine yourself - today reading my book and tomorrow on death row? Unfathomable isn't it? But it is an increasing reality for so many African American males and a handful of females.

Is There Still Hope?

Stanley "Tookie" Williams is said to be cofounder of the CRIPS, a street organization started in South Central Los Angelos, California. Currently, he sits on San Quentin's death row for the murder of four people. At 45, Mr. Williams has been on death row for 19 years. He has apologized to the world as he witnessed the spread of the CRIPS to 42 states and South Africa. He has told children and others over and over that gang life is not the glitz and glamour it may appear to be. He has warned gang members that peace is better than war.

While incarcerated Mr. Williams has devoted his life to anti-gang education. Mr. Williams wrote a series of children's books called *"Tookie Speaks Out Against Gang Violence."* He is also the creator of the Internet Project for Street Peace, a program that links at-risk youth around the world through Internet e-mails and chat groups, enabling them to share their experiences of transforming their lives. Mario Fehr of the Swiss Parliament noticed and nominated him for the 2001 Nobel Peace Prize. Yet, with very little help and assistance, he has transformed his life from that of gang banger to death row inmate to an accomplished author and now a Noble Peace Prize nominee!

Tookie's life is a testament to the fact that it's not always where you start but where you end. Tookie said, *"For a long time I shied away from my own redemption. I was worried what others would think of me. Would they think Tookie had gone soft? That was my concern. I used to think that not to gang bang was a sign of weakness. Many of today's youth feel as I did in the past. But now I know better. A legitimate redemptive effort to change yourself takes arduous discipline to succeed. So making a positive transition in your life is a sign of strength, never weakness."*

If You Are Presently Incarcerated

Read the *Autobiography of Malcolm X.* You will see how he made his prison cell a university. Malcolm read and studied and studied and read. Malcolm X rose up to be one of the most prolific speakers and advocates for human rights, especially for African people worldwide. Read the Scriptures daily. There is so much wisdom and instruction in them. **Transformation comes with renewing your mind. When your mind is free, your true freedom begins**.

In Conclusion

The imminent African American psychologist, Dr. Na'im Akbar brings this whole chapter into perspective: *"The vast majority of creative minds who are males are locked away during their most productive years. In the years when most Euro-American males are present in universities, colleges and training institutes, gaining the skills that are necessary to insure that they can run the world the way that they have been running the world; our future leaders, future learners, future advocates, future directors, can be found in the jails of America, locked away, unable to think; under the daily watchful eye of sick minds who would rather see them dead than learning! Those who show the greatest promise of thinking, self-direction, understanding, comprehension, are least likely to ever get paroled. They are removed, not by physical death, but institutional death."*

Is a playa' still a playa' after the judge says, "Life without parole?" Is a playa' still a playa' on death row? Prison is not a Playa's Paradise? Not by a long shot.

Chapter Sources
• The Sentencing Project (www.sentencingproject.org)
• Western Prison Project (www.westernprisonproject.org)
• Joint Center/Political & Economic Studies (www.jointctr.org)
• Prison MoratoriumProject (www.nomoreprisons.org)
• ACLU (www.aclu.org)
• Stop Prison Rape, Inc. (www.igc.apc.org/spr)
• Families Against Mandatory Minimum Foundation - (www.famm.org)
• New York Times, FBI, U.S. Department of Justice
• Earl Ofari Hutchinson, <u>Black Women Behind Bars</u> (Article)
• Final Call (12/26/00)

Bounce To This!

"He had everything he needed, but he wanted more. And when he got what he wanted, he lost what he had!"

I love African proverbs. I love talking to elders (senior citizens) in the church and community. I wait for that certain look in their eyes - I know it's coming - then bam! - *the wisdom of the elders.* Sometimes it's a personal experience. Sometimes it's just one sentence. I love wisdom. The most wisdom some youngins know is a wisdom tooth! When they get that pulled, they have no wisdom left! (That was a joke I just made up!)

Wisdom is vastly different from a perspective, an opinion, advice, or experience. You will probably hear in your lifetime that "experience is the best teacher." Well I disagree. There are things that you should never experience as a child, youth or adult. My wife's brother, was right when he said, **"Experience is not the best teacher. Wisdom is the best teacher. Wisdom is the ability to use knowledge appropriately. Experience is the costliest teacher."**

You don't have to experience getting locked up to realize that doing something stupid ain't cool. You don't have to experience HIV before you conclude that promiscuity isn't where it's at. You don't have to experience living in a wheelchair the rest of your life before you realize that gang bangin' ain't it. Wisdom can tell you all that! Not all experiences are bad. Experience has its place, but wisdom should have first place.

I hear some youngins say to adults, "You made your mistakes, let me make mine!" I know what they're trying to say, but the responsibility of wisdom is to help you avoid mistakes. Your mistakes could be fatal! But let me get back to the elders. I think the saddest word that comes to mind for some elders is *regret.* Some of the elders talk (as if it happened just yesterday) about their days of youth and how they made some life-altering decisions that they deeply regret. Most of their regrets have to do with their associations. I might have said it earlier but I'll say it again because it's worth repeating. The African proverb says, *"If I want to know who you are, I must look at your friends."*

You need wisdom to choose your friends well. You can't go on looks-or-clothes-or-their cars-or anything else. One of the better definitions for wisdom is, *"the ability to discern inner qualities and relationships."* If you are not careful, some people will seriously slow your roll. *An unexpected pregnancy / a drug addiction / a prison term / a bad choice for marriage / a venereal disease / a school suspension / an overdose /* You need wisdom.

You need wisdom to make good choices - period. You are making choices that will affect the rest of your life. Some choices become permanent. Once they're made, you can't change them. For instance, high school. If you don't work up to your potential, once you graduate, you can't change your performance in high school. It becomes part of your permanent record. I did not work up to my potential when I was in high school. I had what we called back in the day, "a basketball jones." I ate, drank and slept basketball! I did o.k. in school, but I know I could have done better. I chose to let basketball rule. Now I can't change it. It's too late.

My daughters, Porsche and Shalisha are members of the National Honor Society. My nieces, Gayle and LaJoya are members of the National Honor Society. They made the right choice of academic excellence, and they were rewarded for it. I should have been inducted in the National Honor Society when I was in high school, but I didn't choose to work at my potential. I'm not saying that everyone will be in the NHS, but you know when you are not working up to your potential.

I put bouncing a basketball before wisdom. Now I can't change my choice. **If you are going to "bounce' to something, bounce to this: Wisdom!**

King Solomon talked a lot about wisdom. In fact, it was his favorite theme, and he had his reasons. Solomon said, *"Wisdom is the principle thing, therefore, get wisdom, and in your pursuit of wisdom, get understanding"* (Proverbs 4:7).

Solomon's story is fascinating. As a young man, he was challenged by Yahweh to chart his own future. (This story is in 1 Kings chapter 3 in the Scriptures. I want you to read the whole chapter in your spare time.) Yahweh speaks to Solomon in a dream: *"Ask, what shall I give thee?" Solomon, what do you want from me?"* Young people, just like king Solomon, your future lies blank before you, ready to receive what you choose to write on the line of that blank check, but once written, it is indelible.

If you could envision the possibilities of your youth, and the issues that hang on your early choices, as clearly as you will see them someday, there would be fewer wasted hours and days in your life. In youth your future is generally decided. If you go wrong, it is not easy to be set right. You may be able to recover, but it will not be without a struggle.

What do you really want? Be honest. *Is it a choice between vanity or virtue? / Between pleasure or principle? / Between materialism or a mission in life?* You may not see or hear Yahweh, but the question is still fresh - *"What do you really want?"* It is here, that you must know the difference between your needs and your wants and keep them in their proper place.

Solomon trembles to think that he can ask Yahweh for earthly pleasures and prosperity or he may choose character and righteousness. Solomon's reply showed the attitude with which he entered into this critical phase of his life. He is serious and cleareyed as he sizes up the responsibilities before him. His responsibilities, not his desires were uppermost in his young mind.

Solomon asked Yahweh for WISDOM, an attentive mind, and the ability to discern good from evil. It is not intellect or brilliancy that Solomon requested, but wisdom. Some of you envy people who are brilliant, but if you have and use the gift of wisdom, they are not even in your league!

Is that your final answer Solomon? Yes. Now listen to Yahweh's reply to Solomon: *"Since you have asked for wisdom instead of wealth or a long life or the death of your enemies, I will give you what you have asked for. I will give you wisdom and the ability to decide between right and wrong more than anyone has had or will have in the future. Besides that, I will give you what you did not ask for. I will give you such wealth and honor that no king can be compared to you. If you walk in My ways, keep My commandments and obey my laws as your father David did, I will also give you a long and healthy life"* (1 Kings 3:11-14).

Solomon not only got his request but he received what he did not even ask for! His not asking for material things was the very reason he obtained it. When Solomon asked only for wisdom, Yahweh gave him riches and honor too. When Yahweh is pleased with our requests, He gives us more than we asked, and widens our sincere desire by His overlapping blessings.

There is nothing wrong with the honest acquisition of material things, but it will take wisdom to keep your hips out of debt! My point is that it takes a focused, spiritual-minded person to ask only what he or she needs to accomplish a task and nothing more.

I did some research on Solomon. He owned forty solid gold chariots. He had a swimming pool six hundred feet long and fifty feet deep. He never wore the same clothes twice. Solomon loved music so much that he had a walking choir. Wherever he went, they walked behind him singing. It was live, not Memorex!

Solomon had everything he needed but he wanted more, and when he got what he wanted, he lost what he had! Solomon deviated from strict integrity. That means, he got self-centered and started trippin'. Solomon went on to say in Ecclesiastes 2: *"I applied myself to search for understanding about everything in the universe / I tried to be merry all the time and enjoy myself to the full, but I found this was futile, for it is silly to be laughing all the time / I started drinking / I acquired servants / I possessed more herds and flocks than anyone before me / I bought houses and planted vineyards / I dug swimming pools / I gathered gold and silver / I had many beautiful women - 700 wives and 300 ladies in waiting / Whatever my eyes desired I acquired or took it / I did not withhold myself from any pleasure!"* His mad search went on and on until he finally concluded,

"All is vanity! It's like chasing the wind!"

After years of high goals, many temptations resisted, with such gifts as wisdom and knowledge, after abounding blessings and faithful service, Solomon became a fool! Solomon wasted a good portion of his life in lavish self indulgence. But by the grace of Yahweh, Solomon finally recognized the error of his ways and repented. (It takes courage to admit when you are wrong). From that time on, Solomon spent the rest of his life appealing to youth. His most famous appeal was: *"Remember now your Creator in the days of your youth"* (Ecclesiastes 12:1).

There's a whole lot of things out here you can bounce to. Youngin rappin, tellin' you to "bounce to this," and you know what he's talkin' about. He ain't tellin' you right! But unless you "bounce to wisdom," one day you will look back and regret the choices you made, just like Solomon, and a lot of our elders.

As a young person, you are on the front end of life and you have the best chance to receive the blessings, privileges and opportunities that Yahweh has for your life, if you bounce to wisdom.

The Wisdom of A Principled-Centered Life

Our Creator has given us *natural and spiritual principles* to live by. These principles control the natural and spiritual order of life. If we cooperate with them, our lives and relationships will be enhanced tremendously. If we disregard them, our lives and relationships will be out of balance. The principled-centered life is to bring us health, happiness and holiness.

The dictionary defines a **principle** as, *a fixed fundamental law; a rule of conduct; a guiding sense of the requirements of right conduct.* Principles never change. They remain constant. The laws of nature operate according to Yahweh's fixed principles. You can break man's laws, but you can't break Yahweh's principles. His principles break us!

The laws of nature are endowed by Yahweh to do exactly what it's designed to do and nothing more. Nature obeys its Creator. The sun stays in its fixed orbit. If it were possible for the sun to rebel against Yahweh's natural order and moved one degree closer to the earth, we would burn to death, or one degree away, we would freeze to death. Gravity remains in effect because of natural principles. Humans can temporarily defy gravity with airplanes or space ships. But that does not suspend the gravitational pull. It's still in effect, and if they want to get back to the ground they'll need gravity to do it.

The air keeps its proper mixture so we can have oxygen to breathe because Yahweh designed it that way. If we obey the principles of hydrodynamics, we can enjoy the water and swim safely. But if we disobey its principles, we will drown. We can't break principles, they break us. My point is that we must use wisdom to cooperate with Yahweh's natural principles (laws).

You Need Wisdom To Live Healthy

Seldom are youth in tune with natural principles, and without following them, our health is endangered. Take your body for example. There are principles of the physical body that you must adhere to or you will suffer the consequences. Our bodies are 70% water. That means our bodies need plenty of water. A lot of youngins (and adults) don't drink enough water. We are suppose to drink at least 8 glasses of water a day.

If some of you drank as much water as you do soda, kool aid, juice or alcohol, your bodies would never lack water and your pee wouldn't be so yellow! We cannot survive without water. That's the way we were created and as we cooperate with natural principles, our bodies will serve us better.

There is very little emphasis when it comes to youth and health in the corporate-controlled media. They're too busy dealin' over-the-counter drugs, selling beer and stuffing chemically-processed fast foods down your throats! Have you noticed how many "pill" commercials there are on television? Next time, pay attention to the "side effects" that are mentioned if you use those drugs. Some of those side effects are worse than the reason people are taking those pills for!

The fast food conspiracy has been highly successful. Most people live to eat, not eat to live. The fast food conspiracy is all about taste, not health. You need to read how food is processed. There are so many chemicals and preservatives put in food that it's mind-boggling! You also need to read about meat - how it's processed and the chemicals that are added to it. You definitely need to get off red meat and especially, that pig! Have you ever seen pig pooh pooh? You eat whatever the pig eats!

There are 103 minerals in the earth and 103 minerals in our bodies. Because we were created from the earth, these minerals in our bodies are essential for our physical growth and development. The closer we eat to the earth (naturally) the better it acclimates into our system and keeps us healthier.

Our Creator gave humans a natural diet of fruits, grains and vegetables. *Organic fruit* is the best. They are not sprayed with all those pesticides. *Grains* are rich in roughage and fiber. Roughage and fibers are good for digestion. They also work like brushes in our colon and intestines to rid them of waste. Whole grain breads and grain cereals help keep us cleaned out naturally.

Eating fruits and grains daily will keep your system regulated. (I'm going to get yucky for a minute.) One way to tell that you are not regulated is if your "boats" don't float in the toilet. If your boats sink to the bottom, you probably need to be cleaned out. (That wasn't so bad, was it?)

Some sickness result because you have too much waste in your blood system. In fact, most of you have waste impacted in your colon that has been there since childhood! You need to go to a natural health store and buy a natural herb called *cascara sagrada* and get yourself cleaned out! It comes in capsules. It's not like commercial laxatives. It gives you a soft stool, but it gets up in your colon and dislodges impacted waste. Follow the directions.

Organic vegetables are the best. They are free of pesticides. Vegetables can be eaten natural (raw). That's why a salad a day is good for us. Iceberg lettuce has no nutritional value at all. A good salad has green leafy spinach, romaine and red leaf lettuce. Vegetables also have roughage. They can be eaten natural (raw). Raw organic broccoli and cauliflower is good. But if you don't like raw vegetables, you can steam them. Steamed vegetables retain much of their nutrients. Cooked vegetables are really dead vegetables. The nutrients are virtually cooked out of them. It takes reeducating your taste buds to eat nutritiously.

You probably think I'm crazy talking to youth about fruits, grains and vegetables. But if something happened to your health and your physician told you to eat what I just talked about, you would do it without question. All I'm saying is that you don't have to wait until something bad happens to your health to do what you could be doing now. In fact, some of the processed, chemically-laden foods and drinks you are grubbin' on may cause you health problems later.

The fast food conspiracy, hyped by the corporate-controlled media, could care less about the health of young people. Their bottom line is making money! Look how they bamboozle the children. They have certain children-oriented movies hooked up with fast food places so children will want to go to the fast food joints, eat their unhealthy food, and get the toy they saw in the movie! But there is nothing nutritional up in there. It's all processed, chemical, sugar and salt-laden, "tasty" foods and drinks that are not good for children, you or me.

If you don't personally become health conscious as a young person, you will pay for it as an adult. Disregard your health today and you will regret it tomorrow. You better keep your health insurance paid up! **The fact is that the principles of health should not be ignored.**

The older you get, you will realize that your health is one of the most important gifts given you by our Creator. Your health is more important than you 'getting paid!' Lose your health and you will realize how important it is. Nothing at that time will be more important to you than getting well.

As it pertains to you and your present and future health, if you don't do right by your body, you may forever regret not giving adequate attention to your health. Drinking, smoking, drugs, bad eating habits, unhealthy foods, not getting adequate rest, and the lack of water and regular exercise will

catch up with you sooner or later.

"What? Hasn't anyone told you that your body is the "temple" of Yahweh, and that you are to honor Yahweh with your body and spirit?" (1 Corinthians 6:19, 20). You have a sacred responsibility to take care of your body. One body is all you have and you can't replace it. And keep your teeth brushed! My mother told me, *"Be true to your teeth or they'll be false to you!"*

Health consciousness is more than jogging, lifting weights, doing aerobics, swimming and riding bikes. The key to health consciousness is using wisdom to learn and cooperate with our Creator's natural principles.

You Need Wisdom To Follow Spiritual Principles

Just as there are natural principles, there are also spiritual principles. *Understanding natural principles helps you to comprehend spiritual principles.* If you would take the time to study things in nature, it will open your knowledge to spiritual reality. Take anything in nature and research it and so much spiritual knowledge will come out of it.

For example, Solomon gave some advice to lazy people. He said, "Look at the ant and consider her ways." An ant is amazing! It's always working. It carries five times its own weight! If their ant hill is destroyed, they build it right back up again. If a fellow ant is wounded or dies, the ants will pick it up, carry it away to safety or bury it! The spiritual lessons I gleaned from observing the ant is that we should be industrious, keep our communities clean and kept up, and look out for those around us. We are our brothas' and sistas' keeper.

I was looking at a squirrel one day. A squirrel is industrious, and it prepares for winter. But I also noticed something else about a squirrel. A squirrel is one of the most indecisive animals alive! Get a squirrel out in the street and it's road kill! The spiritual lesson I learned from a squirrel is not to be an indecisive person. I must be resolute in my decision-making. These are just two examples of seeing how things in nature can give spiritual lessons. You can learn a lot about life simply by studying and observing things in nature.

Cooperating with spiritual principles are just as important as learning and cooperating with principles of nature. Spiritual principles are endowed by our Creator to do exactly what it's designed to do and nothing more. Spiritual principles such as, *honesty, kindness, patience, compassion and optimism* will bring you respect and enhance your character. The very nature of those principles can only lead you to the destination our Creator has designed them to get you to.

These spiritual principles must be deposited in your character. Character is like a safe deposit box. What you invest in it, you will be able to draw from it. If you don't have any money in the bank, don't write the check. Consequently, if you don't have spiritual principles deposited in your character, you won't have anything to draw from in the time of pressure or temptation, when they are most needed.

Are you honest or dishonest? Are you kind or moody? Are you patient or impatient? Are you compassionate or selfish? Are you trustworthy or undependable? Are you optimistic or a pessimist? Too many youngins want a reputation, but very few youngins want the spiritual principles that build character. They think other youngins will think they are weak. But the strength of character is greater than they think.

For instance, if you are honest, the very nature of honesty is designed to make you a person who can be trusted. But if you are dishonest, the very nature of dishonesty can cause you never to be trusted again, or you will have to rebuild your trust with them.

I was talkin' to a Youngin one day. He was sayin' that there was so much drugs, sex and trouble in his community that it was hard for him to do right. So I broke down to him natural and spiritual principles, and that the very nature of the principle can only lead us to the destination it has been designed by our Creator to get you to. And if he learned and cooperated with those principles, they would give him the strength to live right, resist temptation, have good relationships, and honor Yahweh.

I started with a natural principle so he could better understand spiritual lessons. I said to him, "You see this grass? This grass is stronger than you." He said, "No way!" I said, "Step on it." He did and we talked for a few more minutes and that grass was sticking straight up again! Then I said to him, "What do you see over there?" It was grass that had broken through cement! As fragile as grass feels, not even cement can keep it down!

Grass has been endowed by our Creator to grow *up*. Even if there is opposition (cement), the very principle within the grass caused it to do what it was created to do. I told Youngin, the same goes for spiritual principles. When you put *honesty, kindness, patience, compassion, and optimism* in your character, the very nature of those principles can only lead you to the destination they were endowed to get you to - a balanced, strong character.

Then I dropped this on him: **It is not the environment that you grow up in but the principles that are within you that makes all the difference in the world!** Young people, *you can live healthier / you can eat right / you can resist temptation / you can have a good character / you can honor our Creator in your body and spirit.* As long as you *bounce to wisdom* and live according to our Creator's natural and spiritual principles, you will.

Strange Fruit!

Southern trees bear strange fruit,
Blood on the leaves and blood at the root,
Black bodies swinging in the southern breeze,
Strange fruit hanging from the poplar trees.

Pastoral scene of the gallant south,
The bulging eyes and the twisted mouth,
Scent of magnolias, sweet and fresh,
Then the sudden smell of burning flesh.

Here is fruit for the crows to pluck,
For the rain to gather, for the wind to suck,
For the sun to rot, for the trees to drop,
Here is a strange and bitter crop.

- Billie Holiday, the famed jazz singer

Billie Holiday sang this gloomy song , "Strange Fruit." If you don't understand the song's meaning, it's about African Americans who were hung on trees in the south by white racists. This was definitely "strange fruit." Strange Fruit, the product of anger, jealousy, fear and hatred. It defies all reason to take another human being's life, and do it in such a sadistic way!

Courageous African Americans like Frederick Douglass and Ida B. Wells picked up pens and lifted their voices, fearlessly rebuking white America for the sadistic lynching of African American men (and some women), and for exonerating them in court.

Unfortunately, strange fruit is back! But this time, African American males (and females) are lying in caskets! Thug youngins are producing and becoming strange fruit! Not only are thug youngins killing each other, but they are killing innocent people in their own communities who are getting caught in the cross-hairs of their vicious weapons.

This is my version of the new Strange Fruit:

Face up. Thick platinum cross around
a stiff neck. Ice on fingers twisted in a
gang sign. Potential lost. Future shut tight
as his closed eyes. Bullet holes powdered over.
They file by. Tears drop on a faded Tommy.
Last hugs from thugs. His body cold as the ice
now stolen off his stiff fingers by a thug friend.
Strange fruit, again.

Dr. Bobby Wright, an African American psychologist, dropped some heavy knowledge in the early 1970's that is more relevant today than ever. Dr. Wright articulated on something called *mentacide*. He said, **"Mentacide is the deliberate and systematic destruction of a group's mind with the ultimate purpose being the extirpation of that group."**

It is evident that there has been a systematic destruction of the minds of many Africans in America in particular, as well as other ethnic groups, in general. There are gradations of mentacide. There is *acculturated mentacide* where some African Americans have acculturated into the Eurocentric social, political, economic and religious ideologies that support white supremacy and so-called black inferiority. In short, they are bamboozled!

But my primary concern in this chapter is the *assimilated mentacide* - the internalization of destructive thought processes that we witness in the behavior of Hip-Hop culture that has been assimilated from violent American culture.

A reporter asked a young African American boy (about 8 years old) what he wanted to be when he got older. His reply was one word: "Alive." Tears came to my eyes as the word "alive" jolted me back to the madness that fill the night with gunfire. This young boy should not have this on his mind at such a young age! Nor should some youngins feel that they won't live to get old. When I hear of another senseless killing, I think of the words of that young boy. He just wants to be alive when he gets older. Sad.

Violence: A Learned Behavior

Violence in America has been continuously directed against Africans in America since we were brought to these shores in chains. America's #1 "violence pimp," the corporate-controlled mass media, (print, music, t.v., movie, video and Internet) has negatively impacted the thought processes of this Hip-Hop generation. Consequently, urban communities in particular, are reaping the consequences of America's mentacidal onslaughts. Unfortunately, among young African American males, and increasingly, females, mentacide is producing this new "strange fruit!"

There is something negative going on in the thinking of Hip-Hop culture that is causing countless African American youth to assist in their own genocide! It's bad enough when this oppressive society is bent on your destruction, but when you are helping them do it, that's sick! That's a mental health problem!

When I was growing up, murder in the community was far and few in between. When someone got murdered, it was shocking! But now, violence is so commonplace that it is almost expected that some young person will be killed today! Tupac and Biggie predicted their own deaths.

On the thug side, some youngin's even relish the fact that they killed somebody, as if it is a badge of honor! Add to that, the glorification of guns, shootouts and drive-bys in some of the movies, lyrics and music videos. Mentacide is real!

The ultimate desire of an oppressor is to get their victims to perpetuate the oppressor's madness against themselves. Then the oppressor can just step back and watch it happen and blame the victims. But that can only be accomplished when the oppressor controls the thought processes of its victim. Our renowned African ancestor, Dr. Carter G. Woodson, said it best:

"When you control a man's thinking, you don't have to worry about his actions. You do not have to tell him to stand here or go yonder. He will find his "proper place" and will stay in it. You do not need to send him to the back door. He will go without being told. In fact, if there is no back door, he will cut one for his spe-

cial benefit. His (mis)education makes it necessary."[1] Whoever controls your thinking, ultimately controls your actions.

As I already stated, the corporate-controlled mass media is the #1 pimp of aggression and violence. Just as water is the staple of life for humans, violence is a staple of the collective American consumption. Jamil Abdul Al Amin (a.k.a., H. Rap Brown) said, **"Violence is as American as apple pie!"**

Look at the steady stream of violence on television, movies, video games, and even pro wrestling. The corporate-controlled mass media has subliminally seduced generation after generation into accepting violence as normal.

The violence that was once repugnant and rejected back in the day is now accepted, internalized, and replicated by children and youth today. I'm not saying that you will go out and kill somebody, but I am suggesting that something is embedded in your thought processes that may make it easier to consider using a weapon or violence as a first alternative.

On the positive side of Hip-Hop culture, there are brothas and sistas who advocate against violence. I give them their props, especially in the face of youngins who think they're comin' weak. They're not comin' weak, they're comin' meek. *Meek means strength under control* - when you can but you won't, when you could but you don't, takes a whole lot more strength and self control. It's the thugs who are comin' weak with violence.

On the negative side of Hip-Hop culture, violence is considered a necessary part of thug life. A thug must be violent or a thug is not a thug, so they think. You have to look like you will kill somebody, even if you won't. But if you notice, so-called thugs do almost all their violence in their own communities! There's something psychologically wrong with that.

Deeper still, youngins are writing lyrics, bragging about victimizing each other! Talkin' 'bout, *"Ya'll gon' make me lose my mind, up in here...!"* Youngin ain't talkin' about going off on the man, or steppin' to the corporate-controlled mass media who is pimpin' them and profiting off their lifestyle and lyrics! Youngin is talkin' about *"losing his cool and actin' a fool"* against his own people! And then to kick it so that other youngins are influenced to react violently against their own people is mentacide - the deliberate and systematic destruction of a group's mind!

But it's different story when you or I are sitting silent and tearful looking at "strange fruit" - somebody we know and love - lying in a casket! Or when we stand outside watching in shock as "strange fruit" is stuffed into a body bag and put in a coroner's car. Or when we are suddenly called down to the morgue to identify "strange fruit," lying in a refrigerated drawer with a tag around his or her big toe!

The escalation of "strange fruit" gives the oppressors in the courts, law enforcement and the prison industrial complex ammunition to justify their draconian practices against African Americans, Latinos and urban communities. Even the innocent in the community are treated as if they are guilty by such acts as racial profiling and police brutality.

Mentacidal thinking leads to genocidal behavior. When do you break ranks with the perpetrators of your own mentacide? Yeah, I'm playa' hatin'! I don't spend one penny on mentacidal music videos or CDs, no matter how popular the person may be. I'm not down with mentacide or self-perpetuated genocide - and you shouldn't be down with it either.

The slap in the face of the African American community is that the corporate-controlled music industry gives all kinds of music (mentacide) awards to those who can spew the most invective, destructive verbiage! Youngin rapin' about crapin' on people and rapin' his mother! And they give him a few Grammys? Wake up Youngins! That junk ain't down! And it's more than "shady," it's sick! Mentacidal thinking leads to genocidal behavior. Genocidal behavior leads to "strange fruit."

Media Violence

There are many forms of entertainment that are saturated with violence. Before I dissect media violence, you got to check this out. This tripped me out! My good friend told me of a white youngin he knows who is so obsessed with "kills" that he has on his computer, as a screen saver, the actual assassination of president John F. Kennedy in Dallas! In slow motion, Kennedy is shot in head and blood is splattering everywhere! And his screen saver repeats this act over and over again! I don't buy the line that movies, magazines, music, music videos and video games don't influence youth. It does! So do commercials, billboards and other advertising ploys. *Every action has a reaction.* That's an immutable law of nature. Mentacide is the name of the game!

Television and *Movies*

The average child age two to five watches more than 27 hours of television per week, and are often not able to interpret truth from fantasy in television programs. As the child gets older, those deep impressions of violence in their subconscious mind are more likely to erupt at moments of severe stress or negative peer influence. Research shows that by the time you become 13 years old, you have witnessed over 18,000 murders on television. All this *kill, kill, kill*, gets into your mind and your resistance to violence may be seriously compromised.

Exposure to television violence increases children's physical aggressiveness. A National Institute of Mental Health report concluded that a causal link between television viewing and aggressive behavior is scientifically established and that television and film violence may produce subsequent violence by providing violent role models, influencing beliefs and attitudes favorable to the use of violence. Violence on televisions and movies are portrayed as a means of solving problems.

Music

The continual exposure to violent CDs and music videos, the more desensitized and insensitive you may become. Thus, you come to view violent behavior as ordinary and even amusing. There is also a merging of "sex and violence" where vicious crimes are directed at females in which the violence becomes "sexualized" ("Hannibalized"). It is said that copycat violence against women and people are sometimes inspired from watching or listening to violent content.

I'm playa' hatin' some DJs on inner city Hip-Hop stations that proliferate mentacidal music! Talkin' out both sides of their mouth. Out of one side, talkin' about "peace and unity," and out the other side, hypin' lyrics that are violent, sexually perverted and degrading! Smells like "hipocracy" to me!

These commercial radio stations are about gettin' paid with advertisement dollars. They're in competition with other stations so they roll by any means necessary to keep youngins listening. There's enough music put out that's clean - that doesn't degrade or suggest violence, crime and illicit sex. But it's about ratings and youngins are just part of the game! Positive DJs are few. I know a few. But sex and violence sells and you better believe it costs! Just stop by the health clinic on Monday morning or the morgue on Saturday morning! Somebody got to pay!

I pulled this clip off the Hip-Hop News: *"Over in the United Kingdom a 17 year old boy named D. H., committed suicide by throwing himself in front of a train. Authorities later found a suicide note containing some of the lyrics from one of Eminem's songs, Rock Bottom: "Anyway, got to go, miss my train. See ya'll in hell...'cos when we die we know we're all going the same way'..."*

All I'm sayin' is that you can't wallow in crap and expect not to stink! Youngins can't put out negativity in the music and videos and not expect some negative results. They created a "monster" and now they are scared of it themselves. If they are real G's, why do they step with all those bodyguards? Why are many of those "studio gangstas" scared to tour? Because they might get popped by one of the "monsters" they created! Violence breeds violence.

Video Games

The psychological impact of violence on children and youth is huge! I'm talking about all children and youth, not just African Americans. Video game pimps provide an inordinate amount of games where killing and destruction affect your minds and desensitizes you to violence, mayhem and immorality. *There has to be a kind of psychological "high" or "rush" that accompanies a "kill" while playing certain video games.* As a result, a desire for more "kills" are stimulated. Plus, they are prompted on by trying to score high. Some youngins log inordinate hours playing video games. It was reported that the two youngins who did the Columbine High school shooting, *"had a penchant for playing the first-person shooting game Doom."*

The video game, *Soldier of Fortune* is reported to be a game about a mercenary who kills and maims humans and animals on a series of armed missions. Mary Louise McCausland, a woman who does film classifications, said in a report that Soldier of Fortune was classified as an adult movie, *"Because its depictions of violence against persons and animals are brutal and portrayed realistically and explicitly."*

The report went on to say, *"Depending upon which weapon is used, the participant can enact gory violence that results in the horror of evisceration, decapitation, dismemberment and victims burning to death."*

The gun industry has been criticized for endorsing violent video games. Another study says computer games endorsed by gun makers are *"marketing tools to attract new customers for the gun industry."* This study conducted by the Violence Policy Center, a Washington gun control group, examined several computer games endorsed by Remington Arms Company, Colt Manufacturing and gun magazine, *Guns and Ammo.* Several of the games feature the guns sold by these manufacturing companies. Remington's *Top Shot* video game features humans as targets for players to shoot at. Colt's *Wild West Shootout* instructs players that *"you are the law and you carry the firepower to back it up,"* and includes a shootout in a church!

Numerous studies of video games show that children and youth who play violent games are more likely to be involved in a physical altercation. Opponents of violent video games say children are mimicking the acts of violence they see on the video games.

One study also said that half of the 13 and 14 year olds are able to buy video games that are only to be sold to adults over 18.

Some of you are probably thinking that you play violent video games but you are not violent. That may be true, but your subconscious mind has absorbed the continual violence from those games. It's on the D.L. now, but it's there. Waiting.

I was trippin' when I read this article in the newspaper. There is now a video game where you can be a virtual drug dealer!

"Gamers Get Fix With Virtual Drug Trafficking" by Donna Leinwand, USA TODAY (February 15, 2001):

"S.L. is no drug dealer. He just plays one on his palm pilot. S.L., 25, a New York City management consultant, is a fan of Dope Wars, one of the world's hottest and most controversial computer games. More than 2 million Internet users have downloaded the game, which is an exercise in free enterprise that allows players to live vicariously as drug dealers in one of 10 cities worldwide.

Players strive to become rich by buying and selling cocaine, crack, Ecstasy, heroin, acid or other drugs. In the process, they are hounded by loan sharks who threaten to toss delinquent borrowers from windows, and armed police officers who chase them. Players also must respond to changes in market conditions, such as a drug bust that inflates the price of heroin tenfold, or pharmacy robberies that flood the market with cheap Ecstasy. To protect themselves, players can use their money to buy guns and bullets. Successful players can stockpile enough cash to pay for treatment at a hospital if they are wounded. To the dismay of the Drug Enforcement Administration (DEA) and parents nationwide, the game's popularity continues to grow."

With all this negativity from violent America, its imperialistic wars, television and movies, music, music videos, video games and the Internet, is there any wonder that some young people act out violently? Even pro wrestling has influenced a murder in Fort Lauderdale, Florida. Check out this sad article from the Washington Post, (Friday, January 26, 2001; Page A-9):

"Teen Convicted of First-Degree Murder. 13-Year-Old Faces Life Sentence After Killing Girl in Pro Wrestling Imitation!"

A teenager who said he accidentally killed a 6-year-old fami-
ly friend while imitating pro wrestlers was convicted today of
first-degree murder and now faces life in prison without parole.
In three hours of deliberations, jurors in Broward County Circuit
Court accepted the prosecution's contention that 13-year-old
Lionel Tate intentionally stomped, punched and kicked Tiffany
Eunick, which constituted child abuse.

Under Florida law, the jurors did not have to conclude that Tate
meant to kill the girl to convict him, but only that his actions were
intentional and abusive. Tate faces life in prison without parole,
although that sentence could be commuted by the governor after
hearing from the prosecutor. The teenager does not face the death
penalty because he is younger than 16.

Tate, one of the youngest adult murder defendants in state his-
tory, showed no emotion when the verdict was announced. His
mother, a Florida Highway Patrol trooper lowered her eyes. No
one disputed that the 170-pound Tate, then 12, beat Tiffany to
death on July 28, 1999, in the home he shared with his mother,
who was baby-sitting the 48-pound girl. His mother was asleep
at the time.

An autopsy showed Tiffany suffered a fractured skull, lacerated
liver, broken rib, internal hemorrhaging and cuts and bruises.
Jim Lewis, Tate's attorney, said professional wrestling was the
central issue in Tiffany's death. He said Tate is immature and did
not understand that pro wrestlers are trained to look like they
beat each other without hurting each other. "He wanted to emu-
late them," Lewis said.

Not all violence ends in death. Some forms of violence cause
physical injury or psychological trauma. But it can lead to death.

Assault Injuries

An assault injury is physical or bodily harm that occurs during
the course of a rape, robbery, or any other type of attack on a person. The number of assault injuries resulting from violent behavior is increasing throughout the United States, even though the
media wants you to believe it is just an inner city problem.

Fights

Physical fighting among youth is often considered a normal and sometimes necessary part of growing up. The first encounter may be a fist fight. However, if the disagreement is not settled, future encounters may include firearms, knives or other weapons. Aggressive, physical confrontations easily escalate to dangerous situations and involve other people. Fighting results in hundreds of homicides and uncounted numbers of nonfatal injuries among youth each year. *Fighting is the most immediate behavior that occurs that is responsible for a large proportion of youth homicides that occur each year.*

Homicide

The primary form of violence that is producing strange fruit is *homicide*. **Homicide is defined as death due to injuries purposely inflicted by another person**. Males, teenagers, young adults, and non-white groups, particularly African American and Hispanics, are most likely to be homicide victims. Death rates from homicide among African American males, females, and children far exceed the rates for other ethnic groups of the same age and gender.

Homicide is the leading cause of death for African Americans ages 15 through 34. No cause of death so greatly distinguishes African Americans of that age group from other ethnic groups in America as homicide. While African Americans are only 13% of the population, we account for 44% of all victims of homicide.

Most homicides are committed with a firearm, during an argument, and they occur among people who are acquainted with one another. The majority of homicide victims under age four, when both the victim and the offender are identified, are killed by a family member or caretaker. Older youth victims are murdered by acquaintances or strangers.

R. I. P.

Spray painted on walls in the inner cities across America are the name of youngins with the acronym R.I.P. above their names.

Every time I see it, I'm saddened because another youngin has become "strange fruit." How many friends or associates have you lost over the years to this senseless violence? *Who got next?*

• The firearm homicide rate doubled among 10-14 year olds during the past twenty years. African American males account for 32% of all homicides among ages 10-14, and 52% of all homicides among youth ages 15-24.

• Well over three-quarters of all homicides are associated with firearms. 78% of homicides among 10-14 year olds, and 86% of homicides among 15-19 year olds were associated with firearms.

The funeral business is big business in the African American community! I bet you didn't know that almost all of them have been bought out by caucasian business owners. They are black-run-white-owned funeral businesses. The bottom line is profit. They know there is a lucrative market in "strange fruit."

Breaking The Cycle Of Mentacide

The most immediate way to get America to stop, look and listen is to hit America in the wallet or pocketbook. America, through its institutions, particularly the corporate-controlled media, will continue to produce and profit from mentacidal material as long as there is a demand. If we would refuse to buy, listen to and view violent content, that would get their attention.

It takes a strong young person (and adult) to stop purchasing, supporting or attending the mentacidal shows of actors, entertainers, musicians and other purveyors of violence, criminality and sexual immorality. I know it's an individual decision but it can produce collective results. Big results come from small starts.

I know that breaking the cycle of mentacide is not simplistic. There must be a multifaceted approach. That's why parents and adults must take responsibility to create conditions where the cycle of mentacide can be broken. It takes planning, time and money. Adequately funding after school programs, recreation centers, youth summer job programs, mentors and rites of passage programs, making counseling and rehabilitation (which include violence prevention/reduction and anger management) accessible for offenders and ex-offenders, increasing job readiness skills, providing training and employment opportunities, are all part of the solution for breaking the cycle of mentacide.

Fortunately, there are some programs going on in different cities, but they need to be increased. In the meantime, what can you as a young person do to help break the cycle of mentacide? Let me make some suggestions in the form of questions. Are you strong enough to turn your radio off for a month? Can you pull the plug on your walkman or CD player for a month? Can you leave television, movies or videos alone for a month? Can you put down Play Station for a month? Can you chill and read books in their place for a month?

I know for most of you, you will go through "withdrawal symptoms" because America has made you addicted to crime, violence and illicit sexual activity, but so be it! America is the world's biggest mentacide dealer! How else will you break the cycle of *the deliberate and systematic destruction of a group's mind, with the ultimate purpose being the extirpation of that group?*

You've got to get mentacide out your system (thought processes) if you expect to break the cycle (habit) America has given you for listening, viewing and enjoying crime, violence and illicit sexual activity in the media. That's why the negativity in Hip-Hop culture is so rampant.

Be honest - if there was no crime, violence or illicit sexual activity in a movie, many of you would think that movie was boring! That's because America has put blood in your mouths! What do I mean by blood in your mouths? Female tigers put the blood of her "kill" on her nipples so when her baby tigers drink her milk they get the taste of blood in their mouths. They become accustom to blood in their mouths. That eventually makes their killing of other animals easier and more vicious.

Likewise, the corporate-controlled media has put blood in your mouths ever since you were babies! It started with the violent cartoons. Children are force-fed this mentacide diet every day! It affects their thinking. They see how the so-called "good guys" solve all their problems with, guess what? *Violence.* Is it any wonder that you became accustomed to violence at an early age?

Changing Your Daily Diet

You can break the cycle of mentacide in your thinking and community by replacing the negative with the positive. I challenge all you youngins to chill off music, movies, videos and video games for a month and read through the book of Proverbs in the Scriptures. Solomon drops some deep African wisdom in Proverbs. Don't rush. Take your time as you read through each chapter. Take a moment and cogitate on each verse and think it through. Then apply that wisdom to your every day life.

If you want to lose the "weight" of negativity that is in your thinking and behavior, you must change your diet. Diet is not only what you eat. Whatever goes into your eyes and ears is your diet also. Check out your "music" diet. How much "violent calories" or "sexually explicit calories" are you taking in every day? Some youngins listen to music from the time you get up until the time you go to bed. Got to have your music! But what are you feeding you? Is it all positive or mostly negative?

How about your "movie and video" diet? What is the content that you are feeding on? Violence? Illicit sexual activity? Crime? Killing? Demonic activity? What goes in is going to come out - sooner or later. It's hard to entertain that kind of negativity and not become affected by it in some way or another. Most people act on the stuff they process in their thinking. Behavior is simply thoughts in action.

I know some of you ain't feelin' me right now because I'm playa' hatin' your negative daily diets. I'm just tryin' to trim the fat off your thought processes so you can see clearly enough to recognize how much of an effect mentacide has had on you. *Something is wrong when you don't have a problem digesting violence, crime, killing and illicit sexual activity from your music, music videos, movies or video games.*

How can I say that? Let's use this example. When you digest a distorted concepts of life, especially from the media or negative associations, your relationships with males or females will be affected. The reason some youngins can commit cold-blooded violence is because they have a distorted concept of the sanctity of life.

You were created for moral excellence, not mentacide. You are to enhance life, not produce "strange fruit!" Can you imagine how much peace, love and productivity there would be if all youngins chilled off your negative diets while you read through the book of Proverbs? Now add all the adults to this diet change and society would be transformed in a month!

Cleanse your system! Youngins are constipated! You got too much crap in your system! Have you ever heard of a colonic. That's a way of getting waste out of your colon. Some sickness are the result of too much waste in our bloodstream. That's why it's good to have a cleansing periodically to get the excess waste out of us.

You must recognize that there is too much negativity in your system (thought processes), and you need to clean it out! It's possible. I know it is because I had to do it too! You can wean yourself off negativity by replacing your negative diet with a positive diet. Following King solomon's wisdom in the book of Proverbs is an excellent place to start to change your thinking and reorganize your taste buds.

Another way to break the cycle of mentacide is to become active in your community. Exchange negative activities with positive activities. You can join an organization that advocates and educates people about the mentacidal effects of violence. I have a friend who works with an organization in Charlotte, North Carolina called, M.O.M. (Mothers Of Murdered Children). They are doing a good work, helping to reduce violence in that city.

Violence is a learned behavior. M.O.M. and other viable organizations around the nation, (maybe in your city), are making a difference by teaching children and youth alternatives to crime and violence. They are empowering youth with the knowledge and skills to settle disagreements, manage their anger, and resolve conflicts without resorting to violence. You've got to fulfill your purpose in life. You can't do that locked down or lying face up in a casket. You've got to protect your future.

If you would just stop purchasing and supporting violent and immoral content and become active in your community, assisting and uplifting children and youth, you can help decrease the demand for violence in America. You will also see that it's not about changing violent America, but it's really about changing one person at a time, starting with yourself. These are a few ways to break the cycle of mentacide. After all, aren't you tired of seeing so many of your friends become "strange fruit?" If your are, then do something about it!

Chapter Sources
The Miseducation Of The Negro
Drugs, Alcohol and Tobacco (Meeks, Heit & Page)
Deadly Consequences, (Prothrow-Stith & Weissman)
Center For Disease Control (CDC)

It's On!

"Put your hands in the air, now wave 'em like you just don't care!"

This is the last thing I'm playa' hatin' in this book! How can you let someone tell you to *"act like you just don't care,"* and you do what they say? Put your hands down! After reading about / *young people contracting HIV/AIDS at alarming rates / the escalating youth prison population / the spiraling drug addiction among youth / the increase in violence / date rape / police brutality and racial profiling / the countless, unnecessary deaths of youngins killing youngins /* how can you not care?

Hip-Hop artist have to do more than rap about the problems. And you have to do more than listen to them rap about the problems. Your generation has the challenge, genius, ability and opportunity to do something about them! You can keep your clothes, hair styles, Africentrism, self-determination, political awareness, etc., but you can't afford to act like you just don't care!

You can't let a group of negative brothas and sistas give your people who - *sacrificed / bled / died / marched / boycotted / fought in wars / continue to struggle for civil and human rights /* so that you can enjoy the fruit of their labors - you shouldn't give them the slightest impression that your generation just don't care about anybody but yourselves!

In the Scriptures there is a story about a brotha who cared enough to do something (Luke 10: 30-37). Here's the story:

"A man was taking a trip which went through a dangerous area. While traveling, he was attacked by a gang of thieves, who beat him down, took his money, stripped him of his clothes, and left him half dead. A priest happened to be traveling that same road. When he came to the place where the injured man was lying, he didn't stop and help, but kept going. Later that day, another man came down that same road, stopped, looked, and then went on his

way without helping the injured man. Finally, a brotha who cared came along and stopped. He picked the injured man up and took him to the nearest motel where he put the injured man in bed. Then he said to the owner, 'Here is some money. Make sure he gets taken care of, and if it costs more than I have given you, when I return from my business trip, I will pay for it.' Then Yahshua the Messiah asked the listeners, 'Which of these three men do you think did the right thing?' Someone in the crowd answered, 'The one who cared for him.' Yahshua the Messiah said, 'Be ready to care for those who need your help.'"

Dr. Martin Luther King, Jr., preached a sermon on this text and made this profound point. He said that the two men who didn't stop and help the injured man thought, "What will happen to *me* if I stop and help the injured man? But the brotha who cared thought, 'What will happen to *him* if I don't stop and help?'"

I read some disturbing statistics about youth. The article started like this - **In one day**: *6 youth die of suicide / 1,200 attempt suicide / 10 die from guns / 30 are wounded by guns / 135,000 bring a gun to school / 211 are arrested for drugs / 1,412 drop out of school / 3,288 run away from home / 1,295 give birth / 2,795 get pregnant / 437 get arrested for drunk driving / 1,849 are abused or neglected / 2,989 see their parents divorced / 1,629 get locked up / 27 children die from poverty!* This happens every day!

The African philosopher and author, Franz Fanon said that *every generation must find its destiny and "fulfill it or betray it."* I tell young people that there are two primary discoveries in life. The first discovery is that you were born. The second discovery is, the purpose you were created for. That means you must discover your mission in life - what you were created to do.

What will happen to your generation if you act like you just don't care? What legacy will you leave? What will be most remembered about you as a person? *You like to smoke weed / You was a playa' / You rapped / You dressed good / You could play ball / You stayed locked up / You were all about self / You were not a good example to your younger siblings.* Don't go out like that!

I believe youth is a time of preparation! It is a time of diligent learning, academic excellence, moral purity and principled-centered living. I'm not saying you can't have fun or you shouldn't have some chill time, but even that should be part of your solution, not part of your problem. Tell me what you do in your spare time and I'll tell you what kind of person you are.

Do you have the courage to challenge the negative side of Hip-Hop culture? / Are you fearful of what your friends are going to say or think about you for *choosing to quit listening to or watching the denigration of your people anymore? / That you are not down with lyin', stealin', fakin' and killin' / That you choose to live a clean life and abstain from drugs and premarital sexual activity.*

There are many issues that need the individual and collective advocacy, activism, energy and creativity of young people. I know there are young people on the point, doin' the right thing and involved in community uplift. But too many of you are not involved, which makes me wonder if you would have been a part of the civil and human rights movement back in the day. Would you have been a freedom rider, riding through the segregated south, teaching African American people how to read, vote and protest for their rights?

Would you have volunteered to sit at "whites-only" lunch counters to protest the laws of segregation? Would you have marched right into the face of snarling dogs and high pressure fire hoses? Would you have been part of the take-over of university administration buildings protesting for the inclusion of African American studies departments? What you are involved in now may be an indicator of what you might have done then.

Although some laws have been passed, there is still the ongoing struggle for civil and human rights. The issues of your generation are */ disparities in sentencing laws / racial profiling / the dismantling of affirmative action / racism and white supremacy / the prison industrial complex / HIV/AIDS / increased police brutality / mentacide / ultraconservative courts / drugs /* just to name a few. Plus, there is a global responsibility to our African sistas and brothas in the Diaspora. What affects us affects them, and vice versa. Advocacy and activism demands that you to have a global perspective of the struggle for liberation.

This is not a time to put your hands in the air and wave 'em like you just don't care! THIS IS A TIME TO SAY, IT'S ON! *This is a time to prepare / This is a time to read, read, read / This is a time to organize or become part of an organized, just cause / This is a time for principled-centered living / This is a time for entrepreneurs / This is a time for productivity / This is a time to find a need and fill it / This is a time of vision and purpose / This is a time for youth think tanks, position papers and research projects / This is a time for group advocacy / This is a time to agitate and educate / This is a time for voters registration drives / This is a time for proactive youth forums, web sites and newsletters / This is a time to be educated.*

I like what Denzel Washington said in an interview, as it pertains to education. Denzel said, *"The path to properly educating oneself is not rigid like university buildings, nor is it limited, like a textbook with out-of-date theories on quantum physics. It can be found almost anywhere. Anything that is a mystery, or an area of uncertainty, is, in fact, an opportunity to educate oneself."*

A Luta Continua - The Struggle Continues!

All you youngins of age should be voting! You can't put your hands in the air and act like you just don't care when it comes to voting. Even when the choice is between "satan or the devil" (that's when politicians are not addressing our community's concerns), you have the option to write in a candidate you believe will do the job.

In the 2000 presidential elections, I didn't vote for Gore or Bush. I wrote in Congresswoman Maxine Waters for president and Randall Robinson (of TransAfrica) for vice president. It wasn't a protest vote either. I voted for them because they are qualified and will fight for human rights, justice and reparations.

When I think about the underground railroad, it was not just for escaping from enslavement. It was a human vehicle of transport operated by those who had the courage, conviction and character to help somebody else be free. There are so many youngins who need to be free from mentacide and negativity. But you can't free them up if you're not free from it yourself.

Hip-Hop culture has the potential to be the modern-day human vehicle of transport operated by young people who have the courage, conviction and character to help youngins get free. Youngins who have so much potential but are enslaved to mentacidal and genocidal lyrics of corporate-controlled "studio" gangstas! Youngins who could make a positive impact on this generation, but their lifestyles, habits and addictions are keeping them from accomplishing their true mission in life.

I believe that Hip-Hop culture, with a true spiritual transformation and adherence to our Creator's natural and spiritual principles, can be the "Moses" of this generation to lead young people out of the wilderness of mentacide and confusion. If there is not a spiritual revolution in Hip-Hop culture, from the inside out, from the bottom up, from the top down, Hip-Hop culture will go down in the history of African people as, "the movement that might have been!" Hotep.

"Call Me A Playa' Hater, But You'll Feel Me Later!"

<u>**I WANT YOUR FEEDBACK ON THIS BOOK**</u>! Let me know what you think. Write, fax or e-mail me. My contact information is in the front of this book. **I'll post your comments on my web site.** I will also answer any questions you have about the book. Let me hear from you. I can handle it - critique and all.

"Gone But Not Forgotten"
(List the names of your friends who have departed)

Other Books By
Kwame Ronnie Vanderhorst

*Rearing African Children Under
American Occupation*

•

Family Matters: Hope and Healing

•

*Smellin' Ourselves: What Men Need
To Understand About Ourselves
And Our Women*

•

Scents Of A Woman

•

Whole Brain Marriage and Parenting